Theory to Practice
in Vulnerable Mission

Theory to Practice in Vulnerable Mission

An Academic Appraisal

JIM HARRIES

WIPF & STOCK · Eugene, Oregon

THEORY TO PRACTICE IN VULNERABLE MISSION
An Academic Appraisal

Wipf and Stock Publishers
199 W. 8th Ave., Suite 3
Eugene, OR 97401
www.wipfandstock.com

ISBN 13: 978-1-61097-944-3

Manufactured in the U.S.A.

Dedicated to John and Janet Butt
whose encouragement in the vulnerable mission task
that I have engaged over recent decades
has been a constant source of cheer.

Contents

List of Illustrations

List of Tables

Foreword

IF YOU are interested in a quick fix for the dysfunctional relationship between western mission and the realities of the Majority World, please find yourself a different book. But if you want a fresh, radical, stimulating treatment of the subject, read on.

As one who has known Jim Harries for about two decades and spent many an enjoyable day discussing missiology with him, getting intrigued and stretched by his analysis, and pushing back at some points, I am delighted to introduce this work of his and to position it with respect to prevailing theory and practice in Christian mission and development.

I am taking for granted that a new era of mission is upon us, and in fact has overtaken us in the West before we were ready for it. This book is "just-in-time" education, or perhaps for some of us, "just-a-little-late" education. Hearing this wake-up call may cause us to weep, but failing to hear it would be much more painful because we would blunder into the new era using the methods of the old.

Harries's call may be hard to hear because on the surface his position resembles many ideas which are now old hat among missiologists and mission leaders; for example, the importance of contextualization, the importance of local languages, the avoidance of a colonial mentality among the mission senders, and the avoidance of a mentality of dependence among the missionized. Why bother with one more book advocating such widely accepted truths? Four reasons:

1. The mission world does not believe these truths have been adequately explained. Fikkert's book on related matters, *When Helping Hurts*, has sold over 80,000 copies—incredible for a missions book. He obviously hit a nerve.

2. The secular world is increasingly doubtful about the value of the entire development enterprise of the last half-century, e.g., Easterley, *The White Man's Burden*. Old development theory is being rejected but there is no new secular development bandwagon for Christians to jump on. It is a great opportunity to think anew from a Christian perspective.

3. Mission organizations and field workers are not practicing the familiar truths we preach. What is routinely accepted among missiologists and taught in mission schools is routinely fudged or even ignored on the field. We need somehow to get these truths to penetrate to the level of our convictions and our practice.

4. These truths became conventional wisdom during the modern era, but the post-modern era requires a rethink. It also allows us to take some of the truths to a deeper level, recognizing some blind spots such as the modernist view of the way languages work.

I hope mission and development agency leaders, including many who are pragmatists, will dig into and discuss this book, though I realize this is a lot to ask of them. They will run into some statements that sound impossibly idealistic, and they will be tempted to write Harries off. However, if they read a little more, they are likely to get blindsided by some amazingly practical suggestion rooted firmly in Harries's idealistic view, and they may realize that the real problem with Harries's view is not that it is impractical but that it is unthinkable. It would change so many practical things that our minds boggle and freeze as we contemplate them.

For example, Harries says (idealistically), ". . . it appears that European languages are not appropriate for use in education or for governance outside of European contexts." Pragmatists ask, "What does he want, to turn the clock back before the colonial era? Ridiculous! Accept the reality of the global dominance of European languages and try to make it as positive as possible."

Harries outflanks this objection by coming back with an eminently real and practical suggestion—let theology and theological education today be done primarily in the languages used by the churches' members. This is affordable, it is right in line with the "familiar truths" described above, but it is totally out of line with the reality in Africa and Asia today. It would have staggering implications if it were put into practice.

I hope that academics too will take Harries seriously, engage and challenge his work. Jim draws both from many years of grass roots experience living in the midst of African communities and from his PhD research in linguistics and mission. He has presented many of his foundational arguments in previous writings and does not repeat them all here. Some of his statements may therefore sound like sweeping generalizations, typical of prophets rather than academics. Jim is a rarity—an academic with a prophetic streak, and my plea to academics is, "If you hear the voice of God today, harden not your hearts because the proposition was not nuanced enough to suit you." Engage the proposition, nuance it, improve it, but don't shut it out.

This stimulating book raises many massive issues for mission and development and it is not, of course, the last word on any of them. There are no "last words" in the post-modern era (except the Omega). This book is a call for Westerners involved in mission and development to engage in a deep, fresh, frank discussion of these matters. Those who do engage with Harries will find that his proposals put them into a new position to do the very thing they keep stating as a top priority in mission—to connect at a much deeper level with their Majority World partners.

The future of mission rides largely on the strength and nature of those connections. May this book contribute greatly to the academic discussion of them and to the creation of a climate in which they can thrive.

Stan Nussbaum

Acknowledgments

I AM grateful to Angela Merridale who typed the original manuscript, to Ben Christine for his work on the illustrations, to Lisanne Frewin for her suggestions and for proofreading the text, to Stan Nussbaum for his helpful input regarding content, and to Marilyn James for her editorial assistance.

I am extremely grateful to numerous people of many nationalities who have directly and indirectly contributed to my understanding in such a way as to have enabled the writing of this text. I cannot begin to name them, but I will always remain grateful for their allowing me in various ways to share in their lives.

List of Abbreviations

AVM—Alliance for Vulnerable Mission

CP—Cooperative Principle

LOI—language of instruction

LOITASA—language of instruction in Tanzania and South Africa

MDP—Millennium Development Project

NIV—New International Version

VM—vulnerable mission/missionary

Introduction

THE INCREASING credibility of vulnerable mission as a serious alternative to conventional mission practices from the West to Africa and the third world has meant that the time is right for this book. This book is an introduction that attempts to outline some of the reasoning for vulnerable mission; i.e., mission carried out by Westerners using the languages and resources of the people being reached, in readable academic form. The final chapter includes a section on "how to do vulnerable mission." It is hoped that readers will take it as a challenge to explore further, and for some to take up the gauntlet and become "vulnerable missionaries."

While clearly an academic text, this book stops short of academic thesis standard. In the course of writing, I have intentionally included only the important references, so as to make the text readable and uncluttered. I trust that the arguments I have presented are sufficiently clear and uncongested.

This text comes into press at a time when the debate on the role of "religion" in world affairs is intensifying. The time when it was thought that the modern era would herald the triumph of secularism, is long gone. God continues to call his people; those who are called ask themselves how they can best live their lives in effective service.

It also comes at a time of rapid global villagization. Communication between peoples, who at one time would have heard of one another only through occasional obscure travelers' tales, can now be easier than talking over the garden fence with one's neighbor! The new world of possibilities being opened up by the communication revolution is only beginning to be explored. "We are like travelers navigating an unknown terrain with the help of old maps, drawn at a different time and in response to different needs."[1] With possibilities come dangers and risks of misunderstandings and of generating harm instead of help. This text proposes various means of opening communication channels to a post-modern generation who want to be deep and genuine in sharing with their global-neighbors.

The focus in this text is on the relationships between Westerners and Africans in the service of the gospel of Jesus Christ. It proposes the need for a new missionary era. It suggests that the Christian church should always be a missionary church and should always be reaching across cultural boundaries. The author draws on practical experience to suggest means to overcome the barriers that currently hamper inter-cultural Christian service.

Chapter 1 is perhaps the most radical, and conceptually the most complex. It re-explores the pre-suppositions that underlie a great deal of inter-cultural communication today, and finds them wanting. An innovative model of understanding of language is proposed, that draws on recent scholarship as well as the personal experience of the author,

---

1. Benhabib, *Rights of Others*, 6.

as an alternative to pre-suppositions that currently underlie much inter-cultural communication.[2]

Chapter 2 continues to look at language use in Africa, and ends by arguing that the use of African languages in education and governance is *essential* for the future well-being of the continent.

Chapter 3 looks at thorny issues connected to development and outside financial aid to the continent of Africa. The vulnerable mission principles are suggested as missing keys that can enable a disentangling of distorted debates that seem, in recent years, to have run aground.

Chapter 4 argues that academia has failed, because of vested interests and translation foibles, to communicate the truth about the African continent to the West. It encourages scholars in the West to concede their ignorance about Africa.

Chapter 5 brings us to theology. Theology is presented as the key to the redemption of the people of the continent. This is a far cry from attempts made in recent centuries to marginalize theological insights in the interests of historical materialism. The role of Christian missionaries is portrayed as that of the salt of the earth, with a vital part to play in the future of the African continent.

Chapter 6 is a conclusion, followed by a section containing practical advice for would-be vulnerable missionaries. This chapter draws on the author's own experience of living and working amongst the Luo people of Western Kenya.

---

2. A reader who is unwilling to delve into complex linguistic arguments could jump this chapter.

Models that Illustrate Difficulties of Inter-Cultural Translation

IT IS ironic as I set out to write this book, that I am writing to people who will most likely disagree with me. In short; according to you (my typical target readership) I am probably wrong.[1] So that is why it seems important to explain why you are mistaken to think that I am wrong.

People's notions of what is truth are not inflexible; but they are bounded. An understanding-oriented people, such as Westerners in this day and age, have accumulated an enormous body of knowledge that fits within these boundaries. Libraries are stacked with books consisting of it and reflecting on it. Websites increasingly fill with the same knowledge. To the Westerners, who read and write the books that fill the shelves and texts that saturate the internet, more and more of the truth is expressed, articulated, and expounded in an exciting journey assumed, perhaps, to be leading to "full knowledge." Pressing on the boundaries of what is known is considered to be innovation. But, I suggest, it is only pressing on the boundaries. Whatever might be found outside the boundaries is considered by many western scholars to be wrong.

1. Westerners with an interest in mission and development in Africa.

Language is a classic visible example of the careful bounded-ness that represents today's native-English speaking West. If I cease to write like this, and instead *pput itt liek fis*, I have crossed into the field of "incorrect"! Can language be compared to human knowledge systems in total? Can knowledge be so clearly divided between what is "right" and what is "wrong" that the West has a monopoly on much of the former? Or has the West defined itself according to certain pre-suppositions (especially theological ones that are these days assumed and not subject to critical examination) that are in reality far from absolute?

That what is foreign is usually appropriated into familiar western boundaries, to make it acceptable, is not always realized. Translation has an important role in doing this; it "inevitably perform[s] a work of domestification" comments Venuti.[2] Because, it would seem inappropriate (racist, ethno-centric etc.) always to accuse foreigners of being wrong, translators and those who explain what is foreign to the West do their best to domesticate what they find. That is; what is foreign is made digestible to the West by bringing it within the boundaries of what is "acceptable." So *aliyenisaidia kupalilia mahindi alikuwa Jumba* (*Kiswahili*) becomes "Jumba helped me to weed the maize" and not "*he was who me self-help to weed maize he was be Jumba.*" The first of the above translations is said to be grammatically correct. As translation manipulates a foreign text so as to be grammatically correct for digestion by western readers and hearers, does the same not apply to its non-grammatical (e.g., its semantic and pragmatic) content? Yes, it does. Although this is inherently difficult to explain to a western audience,

2. Venuti, *Scandals of Translation*, 5.

complex, intricate and involved features of African life in the literature about Africa are grossly simplified—if they do not disappear altogether.

Now—what would happen if this process was not engaged? That is—what would happen if what is foreign was to be presented to the West in all its naked foreignness? For a start of course—it cannot be; what is foreign will not make sense in its full foreignness, as a foreign language is meaningless, and the foreign context is unknown (or else it would not be called foreign). There has to be a process of translation to bring the "foreign" into the realm of comprehension of the target hearers or readers of a communication. There has to be a process of assuming (trust) that what is foreign has parallels in what is familiar. Translation is a subjective business, I suggest—contrary to the claims of some that it could be a mechanical task.[3] Translators constantly make decisions about choices of words; the more so when either the languages or the cultures of speakers are different. If translators were to cease being careful to ensure that the foreign texts they work on are domesticated—the products of their translations would be at risk of being condemned as being "wrong" through being unpalatable.

In this chapter I want to examine inter-cultural translation in three ways, each of which make the same basic point—that the use of a common international language

3. Some consider that in due course translation can be automated. According to Açıkgöz and Sert, "This work insists on the low probability of any future MT [machine translation] system meeting a wide range of translation needs unless computers are able to make judgements, decisions and choices consistent with non-linguistic knowledge that people frequently refer to in their daily lives." Açıkgöz and Sert, *Interlingual Machine Translation*.

for the operation (i.e., in governance and as language of instruction in formal education) of cultures around the world for which that language is not a mother-tongue—is unhelpful.

The first way is to look at two sports—for example football (soccer) and tennis. Ad hoc inclusion of tennis discourse into a football context would clearly and indisputably be condemned as "wrong." If we say that a football player gets "two chances to serve," for a footballer that is nonsense, as he does not know what a serve is. The term serve needs to be translated. What is the football equivalent to a serve? Is it a kick off, or a penalty, or a free kick, or when the goalkeeper has the ball . . . ? None of these really fit, but in a case of translation one of them would have to be chosen. To say there are two chances would be considered wrong; there are not two chances given for a penalty kick. There is only one. If there is no goal scored on the first kick; then that is it! Therefore "there are two chances to serve" could be translated to a footballer as "kick the ball." Other translation options will have other distorting impacts.

Instead of translating an alternative term, such as "kick the ball," a translator may give a more abstract term such as "a footballer gets two chances to do something that is a critical part of the game." Or a translator may omit reference to "two chances" altogether and simply say "sometimes a penalty kick may be awarded." This translator, by bringing such a bland alternative, easily implicitly communicates that he does not understand the game being played, and seems to have little to say.

It is very difficult to teach a footballer to appreciate tennis if every explanation to him about tennis either has to be bland or wrong. In fact—not only is this "very difficult"; it is impossible. As long as what the footballer has in mind is his favorite team running around the football pitch kicking a round ball bigger than someone's head into a rectangular shaped target area bounded by pieces of wood (or metal), he (or she) will *not appreciate* the sense in the rules of tennis. The way to help the footballer appreciate tennis is to remove him/her from the football pitch, put a racket in his hand and give him an opponent to play a tennis match in a tennis context! Following this illustration, the (only) way for someone to appreciate what is "foreign" is to go to that foreign place and participate in what is going on.

Could the same apply to teaching Westerners who have produced expansive libraries that include countless texts describing the rest of the world? Perhaps the only way for Westerners to understand foreign worldviews is to transplant the Westerners into foreign places, put that people's language into their heads (and this takes longer than it does to take hold of a tennis racket), and have them play "the games" of the people under consideration. (Remember of course that even if someone should do this, they still remain with a similar level of difficulty when it comes to "telling those back home" what is going on because those back home have not experienced it.)

We could ask; what do words do in a language? It is commonly assumed that words have meanings. I would like to suggest that words do not, cannot, and never have been able to "have meanings" or to "carry meaning." Meanings are not in words, but in people.

Of course people learn to associate words with meanings. So I associate the word eat with the practice of putting things into my mouth. That association however is not implicit in the word *eat*. Rather, it is an association that I have learned to make. That is, a process of learning or habituation that I have gone through brings an association between the sound (and written form) of the word *eat* with a process of putting things into my mouth. That is to say that the sound (or sight) of the word eat impacts my mind in such a way as to suggest putting things into my mouth. The same word could have a totally different impact (or very little impact) on someone who only knows a language other than English. Words have impacts on people's minds. They do not carry meanings. As Sperber and Wilson explain: "as for our thoughts, they remain where they always were, inside our brains."[4]

Inter-human communication can helpfully be compared to the process of typing on a keyboard, such as that of a typewriter or a computer. Words can be compared to a typist's fingers. The fingers have a force, but any meaning that emerges as a result of someone's fingers tapping the keyboard, cannot be said to be in the fingers. Skilful use of fingers can result in the emergence of particular texts on a piece of paper or screen on account of which particular keys the fingers strike. In the same way as fingers create words but in no way can be said to be words or to "carry words," so words "create" meanings but are not meanings (and do not "carry meanings"). Words can result in meanings by impacting on someone's mind in a way that has the mind link them with certain things, because the mind has learned to associate sounds (or images on a piece of paper) with those things.

4. Sperber and Wilson, *Relevance*, 1.

Whoever has taken the trouble to learn a second language and culture (or has grown up knowing two languages/cultures) will realize that translating a word is never an exact art. Words never translate exactly. In other words; the range of impacts that a given word has in one language will never be identical to the range of impacts of a word in another language. This nature of words is inevitable because different languages impact the minds of their users in different ways and organize information differently using different categories.

Translation therefore always results in a change in the impact, in detail, of a word. This applies whatever the word may be. Even if *referentially* the word is no different. For example, a word that refers to a pen, a fruit, a blade of grass, an atom etc. would referentially appear to be identical to its translation in a foreign language. But the impact of the translation of a word in the foreign language and culture of its use can be very different from that of the word of origin in the original language and culture of its use. For example, the name for the fruit orange is in English identical to the name of the color orange, which is not the case at all in *Kiswahili (chunga)*. Whatever name is given for atom in English will have a comparable impact to English speakers who share an understanding of Newtonian physics, but a very different impact on, say, those raised and educated to believe that the four elements of which all matter is made up are earth, fire, air, and water.

Figure 1.1 Change in range of word impact
arising from translation

In Figure 1.1 above, word B could be taken as being a translation of word A; clearly the meanings of the two words overlap. But as mentioned above, the impact resulting from translation to B will not be identical to the impact of the word A. So then translation will result in a shift in impact. In the case of Figure 1.1 above, the shift will be to the right because word B is more frequently identified as or more likely to impact on meaning further to the right as depicted in the graph, as indicated by the upwards-bulge of the graph on the right-hand side. This shift is illustrated in Figure 1.2 below.

Figure 1.2 Shift resulting from translation of A to B,
from figure 1.1, in simplified form

Figure 1.2 represents a grossly simplified version of what will actually happen in translation between A and B—as Figure 1.1 is in only two dimensions. Hence the arrow (Figure 1.2) simply points to the right. In reality, the shift in impact and resultant meaning would be vastly more complex, and in multiple directions that cannot be shown in a two-dimensional drawing. We can surmise that arrows such as those in Figure 1.2 can be of many different lengths, and can point in any direction (in at least four dimensions), as illustrated in two-dimensional form in Figure 1.3 below.

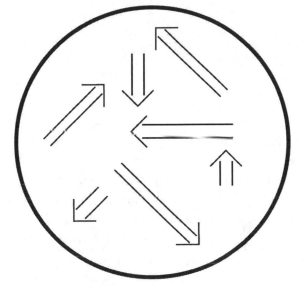

Figure 1.3 Varieties of shifts in impact (and resultant meaning) arising from the translation of different words

We need to consider the importance of such shifts. Are such shifts consequential in the course of everyday life? Perhaps even more critically—do shifts follow a trend or pattern? Do they give a net shift when added together? Or do they cancel out? Figure 1.4 shows a theoretical position in which shifts cancel one another out. If *a*, *b*, *c*, and *d* are the shifts of the four words resulting from the translation of a short sentence, then we can say that the net result of the four shifts is zero, in other words that the translated text seems to be identical in impact or meaning to that of the original.

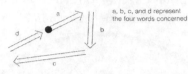

Figure 1.4 Shifts in translation of the words of a four-word
sentence that appear to cancel each other out

In Figure 1.4 the finishing point is the same as the starting point. So there has been no net shift. We can ask ourselves what kind of circumstances result in such a non-net-shift situation.

I suggest that the circumstances most likely to give no (or minimal) net shift are those of translating between languages of similar cultures. Because the cultures of geographical neighbors tend to be similar, this could be between Western European nations and languages, or between East African tribes, or between different ethnic groups in China. The likelihood of a net-shift occurring is greatly heightened when translation is between people of vastly different cultural origins.[5]

We could say that "shift" occurs for two reasons:

First is the particular structure of a language, its grammar, its semantics, its syntax. This is the way that a language functions as a closed unit. Broadly—the way it understands itself.

Secondly, there is the way in which a language interacts with the culture or way of life of a people. In some ways it determines people's lives, according to the way(s) in which it defines categories, and the ways in which its categories

5. Shift is also very likely, if not inevitable, even between neighboring peoples, but is likely to be significantly higher where large differences in culture are traversed.

are considered to be related. In other ways people's lives can be said to be deterministic of a language. *Snow* will not be a part of the language of a people living in the tropics. *Co-wife* will not be a part of conversation for a monogamous people. *God* will not be a frequent topic of conversation for secularists, but will be for "the religious," and so on.

Aspects related to the particular structure of two languages may, I suggest, in some instances cancel each other out. But this will not happen with the way a language interacts with different cultures of different peoples. In so far as cultural differences are real, such cancellation cannot happen. When cultural differences are "real," language *will* have a different impact when used in one "culture" than it does when used in another. The consequences in today's world of some people's failure to realize this are serious. Cultural differences are not eradicated by having people of the two different cultures concerned learn a common language— such as English. The learning of a language does not result in the eradication of cultural difference.

When two people of different cultural backgrounds use one language, then there are at least two choices as to how they can use that language. Either a "foreigner," describing his life or that of his people, can use the language in the same way as a native speaker, and thus compromise on "truth." Or the same language can be used in a way other than that in which the native speaker would use it, for a foreigner to remain true to their culture. (Of course these two approaches may be mixed in practice.) In other words; either the language will be used pretentiously and dishonestly, probably based on imitation, perhaps so as to impress—or cultural differences will be expressed *in the way a language is used.* Anyone failing to realize the nature and origin of such differences will be misunderstanding.

To explain this according to our diagrams above, we can say that inter-cultural translation will have a net shift. This is unlike Figure 1.4—where there is no net shift. An illustration of a four-word sentence that gives a net shift is given in Figure 1.5 below.

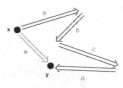

Figure 1.5 Shifts in translation of words of a four-word sentence that result in a net shift

a, b, c, and *d* in Figure 1.5 represent the four words concerned. The letter *e* in gray represents the net shift of the impact of the sentence from point x to point y as a result of translation.

This example of a four-word sentence shows, for illustrative purposes, that a net shift can arise from the translation of a text. That is; shifts that occur from the translation of individual words need not cancel one another out.

It must then be asked whether such shifts are necessarily consequential. No one need be or will be overly concerned, if concerned at all, if such shifts do not have a significant impact on life. They would not be consequential if detail or precision were not important. Sometimes precision is not important. Departing from a friend—whether one says "see you tomorrow" or "goodbye" or "we'll meet tomorrow" or "hey—till tomorrow . . ." might not make much difference (although then again it might). In certain instances these kinds of difference may be inconsequential. In general, however, I think one can say that accuracy in communication is important, and it is widely acknowledged as being important. In this case, shifts such as those mentioned above are important and can be consequential.

In the world of science, shifts in meaning can be very consequential. Omitting just one part from an engine or from a computer, bicycle, scientific experiment or process, or cooking recipe can be disastrous for the whole project. The same has already been explained for the world of language—omitting *our adding ust a fe lettrs s takn ass konsekuentsial!* So lapses in accuracy or proficiency of communication, I suggest, *should* be taken seriously.

I began this chapter by conceding that—my readers may find me to be "wrong." I have already explained why this is by taking examples of sport. My second way of explaining this is with reference to shifts in the impacts of words that arise from translation. At this point I want to explain the second way in more detail—by drawing on the above analyses, using a graphical representation.

To begin with, I want to assume that we have a certain target in understanding. This could be any of a variety of things. It could be how to maintain a car; the best way to manage a market; how to operate a computer etc. It could also be a question needing an answer such as: What is the nature of God? In each case, I assume that there is a correct answer (or there is a correct range of answers), and that there are a number of (presumably infinite) incorrect answers. I want to define this correct/incorrect relationship on two dimensional graphs of x and y for illustrative purposes, where x and y could be used to represent a number of things, such as those given in Table 1.1 below.

Table 1:1 Examples of x and y factors needed in the right proportion for certain processes.

Objective	x	y
Maintain a car.	Level of oil on dipstick.	Level of air in tires.
Manage a market.	Charge enough to meet one's costs. Not over-charge so as to chase away sellers or buyers.	Opening times long enough to allow trade, but not so long as to tire everyone out.
Operate a computer.	Money to pay on virus protection.	Money to spend on backup systems.
Nature of God.	His patience as against his wrath.	His freedom as against his being bound to his promises.

In each of the above cases, either one of the following two kinds of graph (A or B) could be drawn, in which the lines *a* (or the range of lines of *a* to *b*) represent appropriate teaching or instruction starting from position zero:

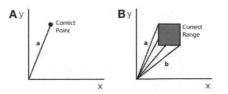

Figure 1.6 Graphs illustrating point or range of combinations
of x and y that are correct, and how to reach the point
or ranges from zero

The above graph A indicates that one point, that is one combination of X and Y is correct. Assuming a starting point of zero, line a represents the instruction needed to give a person appropriate understanding of the most appropriate combination of x and y. In graph B, appropriate instruction is contained in the range between the lines *a* and *b*.

In Figure 1.7 below, the shift that results from translation is included in the diagrams as gray arrows. For illustrative purpose I have taken the shift as being 135° from the vertical. The point (or range) that results from the shift is colored in gray.

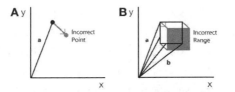

Figure 1.7 Graphs illustrating what happens as a result of "shift"

It will be seen that the original point of graph A is clearly missed, and the teaching that is supposed to be on *trajectory a* results in a wide degree of error. As a result the teaching that is given is unhelpful or inaccurate when translated because of the shift (the gray line) that occurs in the course of translation. In the case of graph B, there is a very high likelihood that the teaching given is likely to be inappropriate. (Exceptions occur where the teaching falls in the area of overlap between the original and the gray colored ranges.) Figure 1:8 below illustrates the direction which teaching must take in order to compensate for the shift.

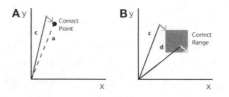

Figure 1.8 Graphs illustrating the direction teaching must take in order to compensate for the shift

In Figure 1.8 in A, *c* represents the direction in teaching that, when translated, results in achieving the target represented by the black mark. In B, *c* and *d* represent the limits of acceptable teachings beyond which what is taught is inappropriate.

Figure 1.8 illustrates how what I originally stated is true—that native speakers who overhear could consider someone to be wrong in what they teach using their home language to a (culturally) foreign people. Graph A illustrates this especially clearly. Teaching the course *c* appears, in the original language, to be way off target. Therefore the person advocating following *c* will be considered to be "wrong." But, following the shift that occurs as a result of translation, this person is actually found to be teaching correctly, whereas people teaching what seems to be correct (*a*, as in Figure 1:6) are actually misleading (as in figure 1.7).

Our particular concern is with theology. Diagram A is probably the more appropriate for theology, in terms of acquiring an understanding of God. The above demonstrates that a mere transfer of teaching of what is correct in the West into the African context will result in the teaching being "wrong." A corollary is that correct teaching (say in English) to the African context, will be considered by Westerners to be wrong. This is why Westerners reading this book about Africa will consider it to be wrong. They will realize that they are "wrong" to so condemn it, however, if they carefully follow the arguments in this chapter.

In a similar sense we can say that, because they receive their information through translation, Westerners' understanding of Africa is incorrect, and therefore what they prescribe as being appropriate teaching or remedies for African problems are also incorrect.

Another (third) way to look at common errors in translation is to consider what seem to be logical errors. One such logical error is illustrated below:

If A=B and C=B therefore A=C

For example we could say, because a man is a human being and a woman is a human being, therefore a man is a woman. Or we could say that because Peter is a football player, and John is a football player, therefore Peter is John. These conclusions are clearly nonsense. How do they inform us of our examination of language and translation?

I suggest that such "logical" conclusions are inappropriately drawn almost constantly in the course of inter-culture communication between the West and the non-West.

A classic one is the argument that because Bill (a Westerner) is a Christian, and Ogogo (an African) is a Christian, therefore Bill has the same approach to life as Ogogo. Another refers to education: because Bill has a master's degree which enables him to perform a particular task, if Ogogo gets the same master's degree, he should be equally capable of the same task. The same logical error occurs in translation in general. Because *mtu* in *Kiswahili* translates as person in English, therefore *mtu* is the same as *person*. Or because flowers in English can be translated by *maua* in *Kiswahili*, flowers are the same as *maua*.

In reality such conclusions are true only to a limited extent. It is insufficiently realized that terms such as these are synonyms only in certain contexts. They are far from identical in every context. In reality complex entities such as theologies cannot simply be transported from one language/culture to another. Rather—they have to be re-worked and "rebuilt" for every language/culture—and always in subtly but often significantly different ways.

That is to say—difference is needed to bring sameness. An analogy would be alternative building materials. Roofs can be supported by wooden or by steel frames. To achieve a roof of the same strength, however, construction with steel will be different from construction with wood. Because a certain thickness of wood is needed, in a certain position, to give certain strength to a roof, does not mean that an alternative means of construction will require the same dimensions in metal. So it is with languages when describing doctrines. The same doctrine may helpfully be translated in different ways, i.e., using non-synonymous words, in different languages.

All the above three ways of looking at translation difficulties conclude that—language is always contextual. There being no non-contextual way of speaking means that the impact of words will always change as the context in which they are received alters. What makes good sense in western contexts may no longer do so in African contexts.

The difficulties in translation mentioned in this chapter have become a serious issue in this age of globalization, enabled by the communications revolution. In prior ages, languages were invariably transported by living people. Adjustments to culture would, as a result, arise by default. People would have to adjust to the community they were visiting. This has changed today as, instead, so-called international languages are expected to communicate clearly with everyone. Whether that communication is effective or accurate is usually not tested because European languages go around the world with a subsidy, and the subsidy itself is frequently sufficient reason for someone to accept the language as it comes. This is an unhealthy position to be in. It results in numerous "wrong teachings."

For a theologian from the West wanting to work in the Majority World to be true to God in what they teach, requires the theologian to consider the shift that occurs in the course of translation. The same applies to someone teaching anything else apart from theology. Theoretically it could be possible to teach in such a way in English that would be considered "wrong" in the native-English speaking world but that would be correct for, say, the people of Africa after translation. But this in practice will be extremely difficult to implement for many reasons, including that:

1. Other native-English speakers will condemn this person's work;

2. It is very difficult to maintain two distinct ways of being "correct" in just one language;

3. Why should someone teach in English when they have had to go to the trouble to learn a foreign language and culture in order to be able to do so?

In reality it appears that—European languages are not appropriate for use in education or for governance outside of European contexts.

Analysis of language use inter-culturally has unearthed, in this chapter, faulty assumptions regarding language and translation. In the past these assumptions resulted in a reasoning being used "in the interests of Africa" that have worked out for its detriment. In chapter 2 I take a look at further linguistic issues as they pertain specifically to Africa, especially in the light of the discoveries of chapter 1.

2

More on Language in Relation to Africa

M OST TEXTS that look at third world development
or cross-cultural mission and ministry ignore the
kind of language issues discussed in chapter 1. This, unfortunately, can make a mockery of that which they are
advocating. Key questions (maybe *the* key questions) not
being addressed undermine much of the case that each of
these texts make. Some of these will be considered in more
detail below. As we so consider them, the above "mockery"
should be borne in mind.

Professor Brock-Utne has spearheaded a campaign,
for many years, in favor of the use of African languages
especially as the language of instruction in African schools.
Her foci are on Tanzania and South Africa—hence she
uses the acronym LOITASA (Language of Instruction in
Tanzania and South Africa) for her case study. Brock-Utne
herself, and those who have contributed to research apparently initiated and coordinated by her, have made many
very useful contributions to the arguments in favor of the
use of African languages as languages of instruction. I can
only relate a few of them here.

Prah considers that "the answer to the language question provides the key to development challenges and the

further emancipation of the African people."[1] He states categorically: ". . . cultural freedom and African emancipation cannot be cultivated, expanded or developed where the language of instruction (LOI) is different from the languages or language that people normally speak in their everyday lives."[2] For Prah ". . . the value of mother tongue instruction is literally incontestable."[3] He points out that ex-colonial countries that have "developed" are those that have put aside colonial languages, especially the South East Asian countries (see below) and therefore that ". . . development in African will not be forthcoming until we start using our languages as LOI from the beginning to the end of the education process."[4]

Interestingly Prah, while an advocate of African languages, appears not to be a friend to Christianity.[5] Thiong'o, another great proponent of indigenous languages, also combines being a friend to African languages to being an enemy of the gospel (as illustrated by his sarcastic comment: "The European missionary believed too much in his mission of conquest not to communicate it in the languages most readily available to the people") and his disdain for the Bible.[6] Compare this with Prah's apparently equally sarcastic attack on missionaries to the effect that their primary aim is not development but Christianization, "unless one assumes that converting Africans to Christianity represents

1. Prah, *Going Native*, 31.
2. Ibid., 17.
3. Ibid., 23.
4. Ibid., 21, 24.
5. Prah, *Going Native*, 26.
6. Thiong'o, *Decolonising the Mind*, 26, 67.

development" he adds[7]—something addressed in detail in this text. It is unfortunate, in my view, that advocates for African languages should not also perceive the need for a knowledge of God in Africa.

Meerkoller adds his voice to those who say that the hindrance to learning in African schools is the use of foreign tongues.[8] Desai points out that "political, economic, cultural and technical" arguments are often used to defend the use of non-native languages in Africa.[9] This reflects a widespread African belief (not acknowledged by Desai) in the presence of evil in their own communities combined with a low self-worth, so that "good" needs to come from the outside.[10]

"The language question is still all about power," says Brock-Utne correctly.[11] Brock-Utne points out that the correlation between "underdevelopment and the use of a foreign language" was recognized as early as 1990.[12] She goes so far as to say that "all the attention of African policy makers and aid from western donors should be devoted to strengthening the African languages as languages of instruction, especially in basic education" as people cannot be expected to learn when taught through a language they do not understand.[13] Malekela seems to suggest that English is maintained in Tanzanian universities for the purposes

7. Prah, *Going Native*, 26.

8. Meerkoller, *Markets*, 40.

9. Desai, *Case for Mother Tongue*, 47

10. Discussed in detail in Harries, *Good-by-Default*.

11. Brock-Utne et al., *Language of Instruction*, 81.

12. Ibid., 94.

13. Ibid., 95.

of talking with foreigners.[14] Meanwhile though, he considers the use of English to be "unfair" and a "torture" to students.[15]

Puja notes that *Kiswahili,* while extremely widely known and used in Tanzania, is for education used only up to the end of primary school. But "*Kiswahili* could . . . make modern science and technology accessible" he points out.[16] Mwinsheikhe points out that English has become a barrier to learning in Tanzania.[17] But he also notes a "strange contradiction" that "seems to defy logic," being that many Tanzanians expressed their preference for English.[18] Rubagumya finds that "for some parents English language is synonymous with quality education" and that there is a growing market for English medium primary schools in Tanzania[19]—something that he finds unhelpful.

Finally Qorro seems to take us full circle. She reiterates points made by Prah. The use of indigenous languages releases "language forts" to common people.[20] "South East Asian countries were part of the third world countries until mid 1960s when they changed the medium of education from English to their indigenous languages. Today they are becoming part of the first world . . ." says Qorro.[21]

14. Malekela, *English as a Medium*, 109.

15. Ibid., 111.

16. Puja, *Kiswahili and Higher Education*, 125.

17. Mwinsheikhe, *Using Kiswahili*, 129.

18. Ibid., 142.

19. Rubagumya, *English Medium Primary Schools*, 163.

20. Qorro, *Unlocking Language Forts*, 191.

21. Ibid., 194.

The work done by those writers deserves a lot of attention. It is unfortunate that they seem to deny a role for the Christian gospel to act as an ally to their cause. The widespread denial of the role of theology in development activities seems to be a way of trying to ignore most of African Traditional Religion.[22] I will come back to this in more detail later. African peoples' seeing the savior/God in the West would seem to explain Mwinsheikhe's "strange contradiction" (above). This is the subject of another chapter in this text that points to the problems of aid and development-assistance to Africa. It is illustrated by a reporter in the *Taifa Leo* (*Kiswahili* language newspaper in Kenya): When the Kenyan government needed Ksh15 billion to subsidize primary education ($214 million) the British government was quick to offer to provide a major part of this.[23] Would they have been so quick to do so if this had not been seen as promoting the English language, and all that this implies for the British economy?

We can continue our survey of authors on the language issue in Africa by taking a look at Brutt-Griffler's examination of the development of world English.[24] Of most interest in her writing is her discovery that it was not the intention of the British colonial authorities that English shall be as widespread as it is now in ex-colonial countries—especially in Africa. "English education was reserved for the colonial

22. Krige discusses this ignoring of religion by those concerned for development, but "to ignore the spiritual dimension of life is to ignore the main driving force of many of the poorest people in the world," he adds (*Towards a Coherent Vision*, 23, also cited in main text below).

23. Chesos, Walimu *Wasiokuwa*, 1 and 3.

24. Brutt-Griffler, *World English*.

elite and kept safely out of the reach of the vast majority of the population of British colonies" reports Brutt-Griffler.[25] What resulted in the phenomenal spread of English was what Brutt-Griffler calls "macro acquisition."[26] In other words, there was a "concerted drive for the societal acquisition of English."[27] Ogechi agrees here with Brutt-Griffler: "The [colonial] system was not very instrumental in advocating English," says Ogechi with reference to Kenya.[28] "If anything, Africans were the ones who were thirsty for the colonizers' tongue," he adds.[29]

Brutt-Griffler goes on to reveal that "Asians and Africans . . . deliberately . . . transformed English from a means of exploitation into a means of resistance . . . [English] thereby played a role in the anti-colonial struggle that British colonial officers had never envisioned."[30] "Colonial officers concluded that one of the important contributing factors to the opposition to British rule was English education," she adds.[31] This raises at least two important and related questions:

1. Why were the colonial authorities so strongly opposed to the spread of English?

2. Just what kind of resistance to colonial rule did knowledge of English enable?

25. Ibid., x.
26. Ibid., xi.
27. Ibid., 65.
28. Ogechi, *Reality and Challenges*.
29. Ibid., 30.
30. Brutt-Griffler, *World English*, 65.
31. Ibid., 74.

Both of these questions and answers can be related to contemporary times; if the knowledge of English was so harmful to the colonial project; what is it doing to the globalization project? Our particular focus will be on theology.

We can be helped in our search for answers to the above questions by going to a more contemporary context, and to the place of Africans in the homelands of English, i.e., to the ways in which African people adjust to life in the USA and the UK. Singleton looks at "the litany of ills for the Black theologian" with a focus on America.[32] He finds plenty of ills to illustrate his case. Ironically the "ills" he finds face in both directions; the Black theologian, Singleton tells us, faces racist discrimination from Whites, and "obscurity" from fellow Blacks. Singleton advocates that Black theologians must "reassess long-standing ecclesiastical approaches that equate myopic thinking with divine wisdom" so as to ensure that White theological supremacy "continues to be battered with stern criticism, until far reaching changes in theological method are made."[33] Blacks must endeavor to "disenfranchise the White community" according to Singleton. At the same time, unfortunately for the Black theologian, "there is no sincere attempt on the part of the leadership of the Black community to expose the community to the work of Black intellectuals and its significance for the advancement of the community" and "for many Black church leaders the Black theological intellect becomes an ideological thief that robs her of an authentic spirit . . . ."[34]

32. Singleton, *Between Racism and Obscurity*, 19.
33. Ibid., 26.
34. Ibid., 23.

I suggest from the above, that finding themselves having to use English is causing problems for Blacks in America, including Black theologians. These problems are such that they result in Blacks "attacking" Whites' scholarship, and being alienated by their own communities. Blacks' attempts at appropriating English in the way they prefer (and implicitly) the way they understand it meets a problem—the originators of the language refuse to give up their hold on it. Some Blacks' response is to say that the Whites are "wrong" to use their own intelligence in the use of their own language. Such a temperament is reflected by P'Bitek (see below), and points us to important issues in language that scholars at times prefer to ignore—at their peril.

Debate on the role of English as an international language has raged fiercely and continues apace. Crystal's book is almost a classic, but takes a very narrow view that English is the inevitable medium for international communication because of its powerful military and economic base.[35] (See also Phillipson, cited in Seidlhofer).[36] Seidlhofer points us to the debate between Kachru and Quirck. This apparently unresolved disagreement concerns the necessity of international English being rooted in mother-tongue use. Kachru, who vocally denies this necessity, is very careful to use English of mother-tongue standard (i.e., "standard English") to make his case. McKay sides with Kachru; "throughout the book, I will maintain . . . that users of English as an International Language whether in a global or local sense do not need to internalize the cultural norms of inner circle countries in order to use the language effectively as a me-

35. Crystal, *English*, 5.
36. Seidlhofer, *Controversies*, 54.

dium of wider communication."[37] She attempts to maintain this position in the face of gross evidence to the contrary, such as that she herself cites from Singapore.[38]

The reasons that I consider McKay's stand and Kachru's claim to be unhelpful should become clearer as we go on. Rassool states that "colonialism shaped the linguistic habitus of societies ... [resulting in the] establishment [of] ... societal 'norms' ... [resulting in the making of] ... linguistic choices that [unknowingly!] reinforce existing societal, political and economic inequalities; and in so doing, they collude in their own collective disempowerment and/or dispossession."[39] Such unwanted collusion has "undermined long-term possibilities for development within these contexts," adds Rassool.

Pennycock cites Carnoy (writing in 1974), arguing that "many educational systems in the third world countries [continue] ... to serve the interests of the former colonizers and Central nations."[40] According to Masemann (also cited by Pennycock), third world education is "part of a massive de-skilling process of third world populations ...," presumably because it prevents children from being nurtured by and into their own communities. Pennycock mentions the dilemma faced by Hong Kong. Efforts at indigenizing the LOI constantly hit the rocks, because real "power" is in English.[41] Opportunities for non-English languages are further constrained by the fact that "English ...

37. McKay, *Teaching English*, 12.
38. Ibid., 55.
39. Rassool, *Global Issues in Language*, 1–2.
40. Pennycock, *Cultural Politics*, 48 and 49.
41. Pennycock, *English*, 193–198.

is seen as leading to social and economic advantage, while learning local languages is seen as an issue of linguistics and cultural maintenance."[42] Reasons given for the use of indigenous languages for education and official purposes are often limited and misguided. Musau is right to defend the use of *Kiswahili* in East Africa but he fails, in my view, to even mention some of the most important reasons (outlined in this text) for preferring indigenous to international languages.[43]

Steiner's telling us that "languages communicate inward to the native speaker with a density and pressure of shared intimation which are only partly, grudgingly yielded to the outsider,"[44] strongly suggests that he could not stand with McKay in her condemnation of the "native speaker fallacy."[45] Steiner's frequently revised substantial volume draws from his own experience of being tri-lingual,[46] and "is a highly informed study in the history and nature of translation."[47]

Steiner warns us that when third world countries run their affairs using English, they are "imprisoned in a linguistic contour which no longer matches, or matches only at certain ritual, arbitrary points, the changing landscape of fact."[48] Because opposing groups appropriate each other's words, but ascribe their own impacts to them, a "polysemy"

42. Ibid., 216.
43. Musau, *Polemics versus Reality*.
44. Steiner, *After Babel*, 300.
45. McKay, *Teaching English*, 42.
46. Steiner, *After Babel*, 219.
47. Russo, Review of: *After Babel*.
48. Steiner, *After Babel*, 22.

arises, which renders ordinary translation impossible, says Steiner.[49] The realization that "language is not the vehicle of thought but its determining medium" was, according to Steiner, made as early as 1697 by Leibniz.[50] In telling us that language does not convey meanings, but creates them Steiner reveals a lot of truth.

Steiner questions the basic notion of universalism[51]— the notion that the human mind can "communicate across linguistic barriers," thus flatly denying the Chomskian notion that any language is capable of saying what another has said. While it "remains one of the most important and valuable concerns in the whole of world affairs," there is no effective theoretical basis on which to hang translation![52] His own look at the hermeneutical motion inherent in translation is educational: translation begins with "trusting" that there is something meaningful there, says Steiner. The next aggressive step is for the new thing to be surrounded by another language. This reduces it to a mere shell of its former self. The third step of incorporation into the extant field (of the target language) may result in neutralizing or expelling the foreign body. Should it survive to face the fourth step of reciprocity, this will result in far-reaching changes in the target language as it seeks to correct its unbalance.[53]

The question regarding English as international language is to Steiner "one of the most interesting to face the

49　Ibid., 35.

50.　Ibid., 78.

51.　Ibid., 98.

52.　Steiner, *After Babel*, 262.

53.　Ibid., 312–319.

linguist and historian of culture."[54] To Steiner spreading English "is like a thin wash, marvelously fluid, but without adequate base [that can be] . . . eroding the autonomy of the native language culture."

Grice is known by some as the father of pragmatics. Many scholars have followed his trail and developed his work. I will look at just a few of those scholars below. In each case, I will consider their work especially in terms of our project—of exploring language and communication issues related to mission and development between the West and Africa.

Leech builds on Grice's Cooperative Principle (CP) by adding additional principles and maxims to define and explore ways in which pragmatics work in practice. (The CP states that: speakers will, in the interests of cooperation, be brief, attempt to be truthful, be relevant and be perspicuous in their speech or writing.)[55] Leech lays down some interesting and challenging principles. For Leech "the felicity of an utterance, here as elsewhere, is a matter of balancing the competing claims of different maxims."[56] Grammar is very much secondary for Leech; its role is to "facilitate the operation of pragmatic principles."[57]

One principle Leech adds to the CP is the Politeness Principle which is there "to maintain the social equilibrium and the friendly relations which enable us to assume that our interlocutors are being co-operative in the first place."[58]

54. Ibid., 494.

55. Leech, *Principles of Pragmatics*, 8.

56. Ibid., 69.

57. Ibid., 76.

58. Leech, *Principles of Pragmatics*, 82.

Ways to request salt at a table quickly come to mind. "Would you mind passing the salt please?" would be a typical phrase in UK English, even if the person being asked is a child. "Give salt" would be a more direct translation into English from many African languages with which I am familiar. The latter could be considered very impolite in many UK settings. A perfect knowledge of English grammar, vocabulary and pronunciation clearly needs to be accompanied by pragmatic language knowledge if someone is to develop a relationship with native speakers of a language.

Leech adds many other principles and maxims under the broad category of language pragmatics. Tact is needed. Sometimes indirect illocutions are more polite or tactful than direct ones. Some "speech acts" such as "thanks" or "apologies" address an implicit balance sheet in interpersonal relations. Leech advocates that we consider the generosity maxim (appear to be generous), the approbation maxim (praise the other), modesty maxim (dispraise yourself), agreement maxim (maximize agreement), sympathy maxim . . . etc.[59] Sometimes it is appropriate to keep talking; at other times it is helpful to keep quiet. Then we also have the irony principle.[60] This says that through engaging in banter someone could (where *h* is the hearer) "show solidarity with h [by saying] something which is (i) obviously untrue, and (ii) obviously impolite to h."[61]

In the field of pragmatics one talks of utterances having implicatures. These implicatures may be only tangentially related to the apparent meaning or impact of a sentence

59. Ibid., 132.
60. Ibid., 83.
61. Ibid., 144.

My saying "I have come for a cup of coffee" can have the implicature of "I have come for a chat." A question, such as "Have you watered the garden?" could be understood as having the implicature that the garden should be watered. These implicatures can be complex: "I am sorry to hear that George and Bill are sometimes late for work." can have the intended implicature of "George and Bill are always late for work!"

In considering this kind of pragmatics, we are far from the conventional questions in translation. Because implicatures arise from the use of language *in contexts*, translation of implicatures can be said to be as much (or more) about the contextual horizons of the original and target languages, than the words that happen to be used to interact with those horizons.

An African example I have often come across comes to mind. In a world in which people's heart orientations are the key to determining physical events occurring or otherwise,[62] certain things are not said through fear of their implicatures being misunderstood. "How are your children?" is a taboo question in many African contexts. The one being asked can suspect that the one doing the asking is planning to bewitch his children: ". . . the Luo cannot understand why people want or need information about their children, unless they intend some harm. As children are considered to be frequent targets for witchcraft . . ." relates Blount.[63] Similarly, neither should one expect an "honest" response to the question of "How is your business?" in many African contexts. In both cases, and many other parallel cases, the person questioned may ask himself why

62. See Harries, *Pragmatic Theory*, for an articulation of this.
63. Blount, *Luo of South Nyanza*, 279.

the question has been asked, and can then suspect that the person asking the question is trying to bewitch the business or the children out of jealousy.[64]

In the course of communication "one device modifies the physical environment of the other."[65] Sperber and Wilson bring into question all semiotic models of communication based on codes, pointing out that the notion that "codes associate thoughts with sounds" is, after all, just a hypothesis. This ignores the fact that inference is needed to link sounds to meanings, point out Sperber and Wilson. Because inference is needed to connect sounds with contexts "a[ny] mismatch between the context envisaged by the speaker and the one actually used by the hearer may result in a misunderstanding."[66]

Sperber and Wilson tell us that "linguistically encoded semantic representations are abstract mental structures which must be inferentially enriched before they can be taken to represent anything of interest."[67] So Sperber and Wilson take inference and ostension (behavior that is intended to show someone something) as primary, and semantics very much as secondary parts of communication. In other words, while words used in language have a role of enhancing whatever communication is going on, they are *not* the primary means of communication.

We do not need to grasp all the details of Sperber and Wilson's theory in order to learn something from it. Sperber and Wilson clearly portray a model of the making of mean-

64. Harries, *Pragmatic Theory*, 50.

65. Sperber and Wilson, *Relevance*, 1.

66. Ibid., 16.

67. Sperber and Wilson, *Relevance*, 174.

ing in which words of themselves have a relatively minor role, and in which a person's cognitive environment—for which one could almost substitute "total context," plays a major role. Words come across almost as a luxury that is not really necessary, but sometimes used. A few examples may illustrate this:

1. A married couple who, having lived together for many years, barely need to say anything as they follow their daily routine. The more the couple talks, the more one could say there is disharmony in their contextual environment.

2. Someone sat at a large meal table looking intentionally across it with raised eyebrows when beginning to speak, has clearly implied almost everything, and will use a word simply to clarify which item on the table she/he has a preference for at that time.

3. When a single boy and girl meet in a lonely place, the agenda is often set before either party opens their mouth.

Blommaert and Verschueren wrote about the use of pragmatics when exploring certain racial issues in Belgium.[68] In the course of their research they find that the Belgian people are struggling to accept the presence and legitimacy of *difference*. (This is a point made much more widely in this text—that there is a need to accept the presence of difference [which seems to run contrary to deeply held {probably unconsciously in some cases} Christian values of equality]). It is also interesting from our perspec-

68. Blommaert and Verschueren, *Debating Diversity*.

tive that what most offended the Belgians about "migrants," according to Blommaert and Verschueren, was almost universally their religion: "We do not hear anything about the possible influences of socio-economic factors on power relations, and nothing is said about any possible cultural features other than religion."[69] That does seem amazing for as secularized a people as the Belgians.

Blommaert and Verschueren take pragmatics as the basis for their research approach. "One of the basic premises of a pragmatic approach is that every utterance relies on a world of implicit background assumptions, supposedly shared or presented as shared, which combine with what is explicitly said in the construction of meaning."[70] Utterances do not "express their full meaning fully explicitly" say Blommaert and Verschueren.

Blommaert and Verschueren determined to try to sort "explicit" from "implicit" and "positive" from "negative" references to (Muslim) immigrants in Belgium. Explicitly positive references to the presence of Islamic immigrants were usually economic—e.g., they provide a labor force— and generic. Implicit positive references to migrants were very hard to come by. Explicitly negative references to migrants were few, as people's self-valuation was that they could respond positively to "others." Implicit negatives were strong. The adoption process for migrants was totally uni-directional; "they have to change to resemble us." In other words, the outcome of this research was to find that an apparent rhetoric of welcome to migrants concealed a very negative perspective on them.

69. Blommaert and Verschueren, *Debating Diversity*, 96.
70. Ibid., 32.

This could have us wonder what is currently being concealed in inter-cultural communication between the West and Africa. The rhetoric is one of concern and love for the poor on the part of the West, and a humble and grateful acceptance on the part of a compliant Africa. Could such rhetoric be a clever concealing of the playing out of vested interests in the West, and a loathing of foreign domination combined with iconic dependence on the part of Africans?

Although of necessity limited in depth and breadth, this survey of some contemporary literature should have helped us to understand a few things:

1. The existence of a body of scholars who are already arguing that it is essential for the future of Africa for its people to guide themselves through their own languages (for example see Brock-Utne, Desai, and Qorro).

2. It was not a colonial plan to leave independent nations governing themselves using European languages. Rather, this happened due to pressure from nationals for reasons of economics and power.[71]

3. The maintenance of English as language of governance and instruction is widely recognized as problematic.[72]

4. From Steiner: the use of English as language of inter-cultural communication is problematic when considered in the light of pertinent insights into translation.[73]

71. Brutt-Griffler, *World English*.
72. Pennycock, *Cultural Politics*.
73. Steiner, *After Babel*.

5. Leech's look at pragmatics furnishes us with additional reasons why even perfect learning of a language may not enable the opening of clear avenues of communication with its native speakers, if the pragmatic rules of the use of that language are not followed.[74]

6. Brief forays into the work of Sperber and Wilson,[75] and then Blommaert and Verschueren give theoretical and practical insights into the importance of taking account of pragmatics in seeking to achieve understanding through language.[76]

Blatantly ignoring of all the above factors spells serious problems for Africa and other parts of the third world today. In my view, part of the blame for this must be laid squarely at the feet of western nations and peoples. Because they have had, and essentially continue to have, the power in north-south relations; they are the ones who should be and should have been responsible in the ways in which they use that power. Supporting the use of western languages for official purposes and LOI in Africa is *not* a responsible use of power. The West has, to some degree, tried to divest itself of power in Africa by allowing local autonomy in decision-making. The way in which this has been done, by encouraging a political, social, and educational system to develop that remains totally dependent on the West, has been, in many ways, a farce.

The urgency of the need to "allow" African nations to "rule themselves" using their own languages has never

---

74. Leech, *Principles of Pragmatics*.

75. Sperber and Wilson, *Relevance*.

76. Blommaert and Verschueren, *Debating Diversity*.

been greater than the current time, because of escalating globalization. The view in the 1960s, when many African nations achieved independence, might have been that they would be able to adapt the European languages they were using to their own purposes. The vast spread of communications technology to date has rendered that dream dead in the water, as powerful western nations take advantage of their linguistic legacy in Africa, and elsewhere, in their own interests. In the process, they force the European languages in use into line with usage of their native speakers. This renders peculiarly African innovation and initiative almost into nonsense.

This chapter is far from having made the complete case for the use of African languages in Africa. The reader is referred to www.vulnerablemission.org for many more insights. The objective of this text is also not to change government policies (although if it was used to that end it could be a worthwhile achievement). This text is making a case to back an appeal to Christian missionaries and development workers from the West seeking to minister in the third world, especially Africa. The appeal is that at least some of those missionaries carry out their ministries using the language of the people they are reaching. This appeal applies even if they work in countries that have adopted European tongues for their own official purposes.

3

Development Projects and Outside Funding

SOMEWHERE AND somehow the idea that one could bring positive change to a community using outside money acquired respectability and then gained momentum. I will attempt to articulate some of the origins of this thinking, and where it has taken the West to date in its relation to the third world.

Philosophers and thinkers certainly share responsibility for the thinking that has underlain "development projects." Karl Marx is a prominent name that comes to mind. Undoubtedly Marx was influenced by many others, and drew on their work to various degrees. He may not have been the originator of the philosophy of historical materialism, but he was one of the proponents of it. This philosophy says in essence that human life, intellect, and society are governed by the material conditions of human existence. That is—the way people live arises from the character of their physical environment. The clear implication of this is that a change to the physical (i.e., often economic) situation of a person's life, will re-orient their lifestyle to the better.

There is undoubtedly some truth to the above, but what has been deceptive is that some have taken it as being the whole truth. Thus they have thought that outside aid, carefully applied to third world nations, could transform them into wealthy nations of a first world standard; and in turn that wealth, in some way, could be fully satisfying. Its many flaws and pitfalls have not prevented many people from continuing to believe and follow this kind of thinking. A classic recent instance is the Millennium Development Project (MDP), which intends to halve global poverty by 2015, and works on the basis that "the barriers to development in Africa are not in the mind, but in the soils, the mosquitoes, the vast distances over difficult terrain, the unsteady rainfall."[1] Sadly, many Christians in the West have got on board with this orientation. The MDP aims are indeed laudable. But it is the prioritization of these aims over more spiritual concerns and the way they are to be implemented (through massive outside investment) that are much more questionable.

The Marshall plan applied to Germany post World War II has oriented, convinced, and confirmed to many the advisability of massive investment into a country as a means to help it take-off economically. Indeed Germany, whose infrastructure had received a serious battering as a result of World War II, made a remarkable recovery. It is the transfer of this understanding to non-western countries that has been more difficult. Germany proved its capability as an economic powerhouse in its recovery from the depression of the 1930s in the years running up to the war. It was not so difficult to do the same again following the war. However this case has proved to be different from expecting a country that has never had an economy (in the modern sense)

1. Sachs, *End of the World*.

to suddenly develop one—just because it is receiving vast amounts of foreign aid. This point is well made by Moyo.[2]

The reason that "development thinking" has survived so long, and keeps on re-appearing, is not because it works. One reason clearly is that certain western nations feel guilty about the masses of wealth that they generate and consume, while much of the globe goes short (even on basics such as food). The implicit moral imperative arising from this situation has meant that it has proved impossible for the wealthy to quietly get on with their own affairs without contributing, often in an interfering way, to those of others. When they have contributed, unfortunately it has been almost invariably on the basis of historical-materialist thinking, as already described above.

The peculiar power of money has meant that such processes of aid provision or development assistance are very difficult either to evaluate or to stop. This difficulty typically arises at both ends of the spectrum—the sending end and the receiving end. At the sending end, institutions are set up to administer the collection and disbursing of funds, technical advice and all that goes with it. Once set up, these institutions attempt to perpetuate themselves. To this end they continue to attempt to justify, by all means possible, their own ongoing existence and role. Meanwhile at the receiving end, there is an even clearer case for speaking in favor of money that keeps coming for free. Protests arise—and from Africa these days antagonists include James Shikwati and Dabisa Moyo.[3] But these are lone voices compared to the thousands and millions who prefer handouts

2. Moyo, *Dead Aid*, 35–37.
3. Reed, *Liberty Blossoms*; Moyo in 85. above.

to sustainable poverty alleviation. As the system continues, dependency becomes increasingly entrenched, and more and more people are forced to accept the system as it is, in the interests of sheer survival, regardless of their view of its long-term inappropriateness.

This system of outside control, in effect, of third world nations' resources, economy, and society is often known as post-colonialism. In a sense, at the international political level, it is colonialism without responsibility. It is a form of indirect rule that the British (for example) would (surely) not even have dreamt of implementing while they still held their world-wide empire; especially because of the way it produces and then perpetuates corruption and control by fat-cats.[4] Because ex-colonial countries are supposedly "independent," external donors do not sufficiently consider themselves responsible for what they do.

The long history of the existence of temples and sacrificial systems in human communities should be an education to social planners of today; people need to find an acceptable destination for their "sin offerings." At one time that was in the form of animals to be sacrificed in temples. It has been in the form of funds for church buildings. Nowadays in the West animals are no longer sacrificed, and many people are not in favor of church buildings (given so-called post-Christian Europe). In the post-enlightenment age, people want to do useful things with their money, according to their rational historical-materialist understanding. They are no longer content to use their resources just to please the god(s) or to direct the course of fate through manipulation of the spiritual realm.

4. Moyo, *Dead Aid*, 49.

This is an area that urgently needs the attention of theologians. At the moment they seem resigned to accepting that even church funds be used, in effect, to fuel secularism (i.e., historical materialism)—as illustrated by the support the MDP has received from Christian organizations. (The Micah Challenge [http://www.micahchallenge.org.uk/] seems to epitomize this.) One answer to this dilemma, I suggest, could be to invest in church buildings in the West. Short-term mission trips could be another—if only they would stop carrying money to hand over in ways that de-stabilize their hosts in the third world. Then there is the support needed by one's own workers—i.e., Westerners called to live and work in the third world for an extended period, who want to work amongst non-western people using *their* languages and resources—a process we are calling "vulnerable mission."

The West's belief in human equality is admirable, but problematic. It certainly aggravates inter-racial tensions in the West, because as a result of this belief, immigrants are able to thrive on government money even if they do not work. The contribution of social-security systems to "racism" needs a separate study, but it is certainly a major aggravation. Government-sponsored social security systems obviate the need for relationships between immigrants and nationals that would otherwise arise out of interdependence becoming an economic necessity. That is—if immigrant communities were not given free handouts, their searching for economic survival and advance would surely result in a higher degree of integration into indigenous communities than is currently the case.

Rowell's recent publication attempts to justify, from a Christian perspective, the ongoing generosity from the West to the poor in other countries.[5] He especially takes issue with those who point to the danger of giving to the poor because of the dependence that this generates. Rowell says, "We manage to convince ourselves that we are 'somehow' acting in the best interests of impoverished people by keeping what is ours, even as we observe their incredible needs." ". . . missiological principles that emphasize western concerns about dependency are sometimes being applied today to serve selfish ends rather then moving us toward a search for more sacrificial means," he emphasizes. Rowell strikes "at the heart of traditional perspectives on this subject . . . ."[6]

Rowell wants to incorporate the best of both worlds. Instead of having "crippled Christianity" that comes without compassion, he wants "transformational development professionals" as he is concerned that "neither . . . evangelism . . . nor development . . . is adequate when pursued alone."[7] He does not seem to consider one outcome of this—that if these two are combined, the model of evangelism and development being demonstrated by Westerners will be out of reach to the "poor"—necessitating that evangelism/development will always be rooted in the West i.e., implicitly (this is not made explicit by Rowell, but is my point) "god" having become "the West."[8]

5. Rowell, *To Give or Not*, 5.

6. Ibid, 3, 5.

7. Ibid., 8, 9.

8. In so far as the West is needed to enable Majority World evangelism, one can say that in a sense the West is the god being proclaimed.

"We are not bartering compassion for conversions" says Rowell, but we need to "learn new languages and master new cultures."[9] He does not explain how someone is to do this when living like the legendary King Midas (who caused everything he touched to turn into gold). (Western people can be this way in their interaction with third world peoples, because of their determination to be generous.) Such a person can hardly mix freely with the poor. They will be pre-occupied with pleasing donors, fund raising and accountability. If they cannot mix freely with the poor, how can they master languages and cultures? (The non-poor among the nationals will typically include many people who have adopted western languages and life-styles.)

"The root of the problem" according to Rowell is "all the strings" attached to giving.[10] But is giving possible without strings?[11] Rowell believes that "the negative realities we associate with dependency can be largely reduced without denying legitimately needed support for the poor," but does not explain how to do this.[12] Rowell attacks the well-known "three self" principle as arising from "greed."[13] Rowell quotes Padilla.[14] Padilla's is a classic instance of an understanding that arises when English is appropriated to the non-West. It then makes perfect sense that "mission" and "wealth distribution" should go together. Hence "one cannot properly help a person by taking care of his or her

9. Rowell, *To Give or Not*, 14.

10. Ibid., 18.

11. Harries, *Difficulties in Giving*.

12. Rowell, *To Give or Not*, 23.

13. Ibid., 40.

14. Ibid., 72.

needs of one type . . . while disregarding bodily needs."[15] The difficulty in this process arises for Westerners who are the originators of capitalism and "the modern," i.e., the wealth that Padilla wants to share out. The Westerners (presumably as it is they who instigated it and still in many ways run it) know how modern capitalism works. Passing on the fruit of capitalism without enabling people to "do capitalism" is like giving someone a fish instead of teaching them to fish! But it is the passing on of the foundations of capitalism that is proving so difficult.

Rowell is one who believes that the Marshall plan offers a model for missionaries and states that "restraint in mission giving" is "absurd" and results in his getting so frustrated.[16] He goes so far as to say that we should "call projects 'sustainable' because they are generating a 'kingdom profit' whether they generate a cash profit or not."[17]

Having made many critical comments on Rowell's book does not mean I cannot acknowledge that his work contains much useful advice. Rowell has recorded many useful insights. It is their implementation that is hard to see, given the nature of people—especially in the poor societies around the world. Rowell prefers to ignore the uniqueness of today's context. We are, frankly, no longer in biblical times. There is no longer an understanding of "limited good" as there once was.[18] The capitalism that generates the wealth that Rowell is so keen to disburse is a complex creature, and is itself perhaps "immoral," in ways that Rowell

15. Padilla, *Holistic Mission*, 15.

16. Rowell, *To Give or Not*, 141, 167.

17. Ibid., 226.

18. Foster, *Traditional Societies*.

does not consider. Rowell's view of history and language is very simple. He tends to declare, rather than argue for, the weaknesses of the current cautionary advice these days often given against the creation of dependency. His writing represents an effort to return to a naivety in international relations that we could best do without.

All the above having been said, the case I make in this text is not that giving should cease, or even be reduced. But rather, that it need not be hegemonic, and some Westerners should be excused from the debilitating burden that is a product of its being a moral imperative for all. This is a "debilitating burden," if for no other reason, because it keeps Westerners in ignorance, while powerful; African criticism of the West and Westerners is always muted by the reality of their economic dependence on it. We need to get away from the moral *imperative* to "give" at all costs.

The reason for the caution I express in the above paragraph is my sheer amazement at the current system. Thousands of people work in that system (Moyo estimates this at 500,000 [19]); millions and millions back it—in apparent ignorance of the serious flaws that it contains. I personally, despite many (but not exhaustive efforts), have yet to find a Westerner who ministers amongst African people other than from the advantages they have arising either from their knowledge of European languages and/or access to resources from outside of the continent. *(If any such person should be reading this book, please do make yourself known to me.)* Rather than try to overturn a system supported by millions (or billions), I prefer to advocate that there be at least a few, even three or four Westerners to begin with,

19. Moyo, *Dead Aid*, 54.

who buck the system. If the powers that be refuse—one will be forced to ask what they are hiding.

Viv Grigg is a giant in the study of mission, with a focus on the urban poor. He has written a lot of material and has been active in encouraging an appropriate response by western Christians to poverty (both in writing and in practice) for many years. (See http://www.urbanleaders.org/home/.)

Reading his book was to me a fascinating exercise.[20] The very title of the book and Grigg's self-definition of his ministry is "orientation to the poor." One presumes throughout, and I think rightly, that his objectives include assisting in removing the "urban poor" from their poverty. Yet it is equally clear that he is struggling to know just *how* to do that. As a result Grigg alternates between advocating charitable giving, and warning against it, in order to give prominence to the gospel. So Grigg tells us that "to be poor among the poor . . . is to bring the riches of rich friends, our resources of wealth and education and power, to affect the needs of the poor."[21] He even goes so far as to tell us that "rich people are to live simply and use their capital to benefit the poor. This is justice. For a western missionary or a Christian businessman to live otherwise is a great evil."[22] Later he states categorically that: ". . . the error of many evangelical aid agencies appears to be not so much theological as tactical. The entrance point into communities in the Scripture is not aid programs, projects, or good deeds. It is breaking down of demonic powers by the proclamation of the cross. This is accomplished in the context of doing

20. Grigg, *Companion to the Poor*.

21. Ibid., 61.

22. Ibid., 89.

good deeds and results in a spiritual change, which in turn transforms social, economic, and cultural values."[23]

At this point Grigg advocates that the focus of Christian ministry to the poor be in the spiritual realm. Implementing this orientation requires an orientation other than to "aid programs" or "projects." So then—is there a moral imperative to "give" or not "to give"?

Grigg defines his ministry as being amongst the poor. Guilt seems to be a key issue to him, therefore, from the start. The poverty that drags people down "is a drum beating in my head day after day" says Grigg ". . . a beat that impels me forward into long hours of discipline and constant work."[24] This is a temperament that I can identify with. Grigg realized, in the course of time, that "most economic projects fail" due to "personal sin and the inability of the poor to manage finances."[25] "The gospel and the Word of God are basic to economic change," he adds.[26] Another reason for avoiding projects Grigg mentions is to "remain free from the administrative and management load that each economic and legal project demands."[27]

Grigg ends up telling people in churches a simple message; "God's method is people."[28] He founded the "urban leadership foundation,"[29] through which he advocates sacrifice, suffering and simplicity of lifestyle to workers,

23. Grigg, *Companion to the Poor*, 103.

24. Ibid, 154.

25. Ibid., 157.

26. Ibid., 158.

27. Ibid., 169.

28. Ibid., 204.

29. Ibid., 207.

who should commit themselves initially to six years, with a view to extending to fifteen or twenty years.[30] Workers should live and work amongst poor communities six days per week, then for one day attend a retreat "led by an older mature couple"—all this after eight or nine years of training! Those who have encountered suffering in the West are the better equipped for work amongst the poor, according to Grigg. Workers must have learned to work under authority. Grigg advocates service as a fitting substitute for courting: "many people give their early years to the pursuit of love— we must give it to the pursuit of God."[31]

The same dissonance (alternatively for and against "aid" provision) evident in Grigg's writing is also to be found in that of Jonathan Martin. Ten years of overseas mission experience,[32] followed by a key mission's position in a large church in the USA, were sufficient to motivate Martin to write to encourage others to learn from his experience. The primary concern expressed in his title is: "How to give *wisely*."

Martin's book is full of stories. His opening story suggests that global inequality is due to accidents of unequal rainfall. Thus he suggests that people are not responsible for their poverty.[33] Martin's examples, story after story, blast a lot of contemporary mission practice. He castigates the church: "government redistribution of wealth seems to impoverish the very people it wants to help. Yet the church continues to make the mistake our governments make,"

30. Ibid., 204, 205.
31. Ibid., 214.
32. Martin, *Giving Wisely*, back cover.
33. Ibid., 18–23.

he relates.[34] "Ending poverty in this world isn't about re-distributing our mounds of stuff and piles of money," he adds.[35] Money can create more serious problems than it solves (even in America).[36] Dependency can be created; the church can be weakened.[37] Martin tells us that the evangelist "paid from abroad" is despised in the third world.[38] "Donated money . . . [is] the machete that chops the legs out from under a man."[39] An angry Zimbabwean says "I have seen sponsorships come in and tell a father he is no longer needed," reports Martin.[40]

While Martin recognizes the problems, he seems reluctant to provide a radical solution. Perhaps he is under pressure at all costs, given his living context (part of the leadership in a large American church), not to say "American money is not needed." Therefore, his topic is giving wisely (and not "giving less"). This is rather like Jacqueline Novogratz, in a taped discussion, with Dambisa Moyo. Novogratz is in favor of clever ways to give aid. Moyo's response is to say "There are no countries that have achieved long term economic growth and reduced poverty as dramatically as we have seen [elsewhere] . . . that have been wholly dependent on the aid system."[41] In my view, Martin could have been even more radical in his critique of the aid

34. Ibid., 58.
35. Ibid., 59.
36. Ibid., 62.
37. Ibid., 64.
38. Ibid., 94.
39. Ibid., 102.
40. Ibid., 138.
41. Moyo and Novogratz, *Efficacy of Foreign Aid*.

mentality by the church. He advises that a potential donor should check out the aid organization he is to give to—as if a typical churchgoer could ascertain irregularities that occur thousands of miles away amongst foreign cultures, peoples, and languages. He encourages relief organizations to work through churches even though he has already said that the worst thing that could happen to his home church would probably be finding a wealthy donor![42]

As Grigg and Novogratz above, Martin does not seem to consider the option that some Westerners fill roles other than as donors. If he is right that western Christians have a moral obligation to give to the poor, does it follow that this must be the identity of every Westerner (American) in the third world? This is, in Africa at least, very much the case today. Apparently its racist overtones are not considered by Martin—in African communities where every White one meets is not only rich, but also builds all their relationships sooner or later on money.[43] For a Christian missionary to so insist (in effect though not by intent) that all friends be bought strikes me as disappointing. (I appreciate that not all will read Martin that way.) In my experience of the areas of Africa with which I am familiar—such "buying of friends" will be the almost inevitable outcome of what Martin advocates. Why is no Westerner ready to face poor nationals without a heavy cumbersome armor of *money*? (see 1 Sam 17:38–39). Martin's book contains much good advice—but on this point it seems to fall short; there is an urgent need for Westerners who will build relationships with the "poor"

---

42. Martin, *Giving Wisely*, 187.
43. Ibid., 74.

on a foundation other than their wealth. Martin seems to sidestep this need.

It is ironic that those concerned for promoting third world development seem to forget that money linked to them is power that they wield. One rightly finds advice given to budding development workers and missionaries—that they should listen carefully, be very humble, allow nationals to take the lead, be contextualized, consider sustainability, and develop close relationships with the poor. At the same time, they have an armory of available money (of vast size in local terms) constantly at their disposal that they are free to wield at any time as they wish. This puts a Westerner into a position of structural power that no amount of (feigned?) humility can undo. Westerners coming into poor communities are immediately in the position of being major power brokers, while also being majorly ignorant of cultural norms. The term "loose cannon" comes to mind.

The solution to the above dilemma can be simple (if also, at the same time, difficult and complex): have some western workers engaged in their key project from the position of being confined to locally available resources. That is not to say they should starve or live in a hovel. That is another issue. I do not refer here to their lifestyle, but to their ministry. This does not mean that less money should be spent in total. Missionary B can take over the spending of missionary A. The total amount of spending can thus stay the same. That is to say, if a western missionary working with the poor feels convicted that they should share their wealth with them, then let them do so indirectly. They can send their money to World Vision, or to Tear Fund, or give it to a missionary colleague to invest into their project. All these avenues, if carried out anonymously (as Jesus recommends in Matthew's Gospel, 6:3 that ". . . when you give to the needy, do not let your left hand know what your right hand is doing" New International Version [NIV]), will not blight the donor's reputation. It will not result in the reputation for a donor of "buying" all the people he/she works with.

If western interests, including churches, do not get their act together on this score, then they may well be hindering rather than helping the third world—even if unaware that they are doing so.

4

What Is Africa?

M<small>Y FOCUS</small> in this text on Africa arises from the nature of my personal experience living in this continent. I consider that much that I have stated herein is also more widely applicable.

Because how one responds to an entity will depend on how one understands it, it is important to ask: What is Africa? Possible answers to that question are infinite. There is no unbiased/impartial answer. For the purposes of this text, we are looking for the answer that will helpfully orient our approach and response to what we find.

Is Africa the same, or is it different from the West? That could be rephrased as asking "Where (in what qualities) are its people the same, and in what qualities are they different?" In our analysis of Africa: who are we trying to please? Is this an analysis to please donors? To pacify sensitive African spirits? To convince Westerners of their own superiority? Where are we standing in relation to Africa?

I will not begin to claim to be "objective." It is probably most appropriate to say that my portrayal of Africa is intended to dispel unhelpful myths. That is, it is a portrayal that attempts to correct miscomprehensions (that result in inappropriate interventional strategies) on the part of the

West. It seeks to address and to rectify misunderstandings considered by this author to be consequential and harmful in their impact.

The view presented in this text is inevitably geographically biased. No one's view of Africa can represent the whole continent from experience in every part of it. My own experience is primarily in Kenya; also in Zambia, Tanzania and, to a very small extent, Uganda, Rwanda, Zimbabwe, South Africa, Namibia, and Ethiopia. Within Kenya, my time has been spent in the West, near President Barak Obama's African home, primarily amongst his people, the Luo, and their neighbors. I have lived in Africa since 1988. Since 1993 my home has been in a rural Luo village, and my primary occupation has been Bible training. I conduct this training sometimes using English, at times *Kiswahili*, and at other times *Dholuo*.

One consideration that constantly frustrates attempts at answering the question "What is Africa?" is the language in use here. Western English (and I presume my reader to be a Westerner) is rooted in a western context and culture, so how can it possibly be used to describe something outside of that context and culture? In short: it cannot. What it can do, in its articulation of "the other," is to imply ways in which the West ought (or ought not) to relate to it. Such "implications" (or implicatures) are far from objective. There is no way, I suggest, of separating one's interest from one's analyses. In my years of living on the continent, I have become increasingly concerned that the analysis by the West of Africa is, in some serious ways, unhelpful.

I will begin by examining some authors on Africa who have unhesitatingly identified difference. I do so while recognizing that western scholarship overall either has not necessarily recognized that difference, or has not taken it seriously. This is, at least in part, because scholars can fail to find terms and phrases in English that are sufficiently startling to mark cultural differences. As a result western scholarship can brush over differences—and this is indeed what frequently happens.

Evans-Pritchard, one of the great figures in the history of anthropology, is renowned for his classic entitled *Witchcraft, Oracles and Magic among the Azande.*[1] Before looking further at Zande witchcraft, I want to consider Evans-Pritchard's view of Zande theology. Evans-Pritchard points out that missionaries can make the same logical error I highlighted on page 17: "The assumption is that because the Azande invoke Mbori in a way that resembles our [western Christians'] prayers to God they have a theistic doctrine similar to ours" says Evans-Pritchard.[2] Evans-Pritchard attempts to make a case for the Zande (a Sudanese people) being *different* from the expectations of western missionaries and theologians. Perhaps unfortunately, Evans-Pritchard's account coming across as an attack on theology might have reduced its role in provoking discussion amongst beleaguered theologians.

Evans-Pritchard's explanation, on the Zande practices related to witchcraft, is striking.[3] Taking such explanations along with other texts such as Melland's, one would have thought it would be clear that African people are entrenched

---

1. Evans-Pritchard, *Witchcraft, Oracles and Magic.*
2. Evans-Pritchard, *Zande Theology*, 39.
3. Evans-Pritchard, *Witchcraft, Oracles and Magic.*

in witchcraft.[4] Haar is able to draw a conclusion to this effect. In the book she edited, she collated contributions from around the continent that clearly demonstrate the ongoing prevalence of witchcraft.[5] Witchcraft can apprehend globalization or modernity, explains Ellis.[6] Witchcraft beliefs tend to be bracketed or put aside by western scholars (according to Akrong[7]), who do not know what to do with them, but these beliefs are no less real as a result. Contrary to the popular view that they will disappear when economies advance, "economic well-being and disaster" can both result in a *rise* in witchcraft beliefs.[8] Bongmba explains that witchcraft "continues to divide families and drive a wedge between communities."[9] Changes in African societies "have not succeeded in changing people's beliefs concerning these mystical forces" according to Danfulani.[10] Witchcraft is a "reality which needs to be taken seriously."[11] Witchcraft accusations in Ghana destroy "community life."[12] Unless witchcraft is faced, "many projects and investments, especially in rural areas, are bound to fail" according to Hinfelaar (with reference to Zambia).[13] Nyaga appears to agree, as "witchcraft beliefs and practices pose serious constraints to community

4. Melland, *In Witch Bound Africa*.

5. Haar, *Imagining Evil*.

6. Ellis, *Witching-times*.

7. Akrong, *Phenomenology*, 57–58.

8. Dovlo, *Witchcraft in Contemporary Ghana*, 69.

9. Bongmba, *Witchcraft*, 122–23.

10. Danfulani, *Anger as a Metaphor*, 181.

11. Mbambo, *Mbambi Brought the Message*, 186.

12. Ntloedibe-Kuswana, *Witchcraft as a Challenge*, 225.

13. Hinfelaar, *Witch-hunting in Zambia*, 229.

development" in Tanzania.[14] Kgatla tells us that, "for Black South Africans to develop after the demise of apartheid, it is imperative to find an urgent and lasting solution to the carnage caused by witch-pointing."[15] Van Beek notes, with distress, that "anyone opposing it [witchcraft] is prone to accusation."[16] All in all we can conclude: witchcraft is both widespread, and powerful in its impact, over much of the African continent.

I am privileged to have access to the writings of Mboya through my knowledge of the Luo language. (One of his classic texts has now been translated into English.)[17] Mboya is clear in his view of the importance of a people having knowledge of their own traditions and history in order for them to advance.[18] In his book on *chira*, he explains that the Luo people's failure to follow Luo customs will result in disaster for them.[19] There is no doubt at all in Mboya's mind that his people, the Luo, are a singular people with unique beliefs. For him as an individual, that implies their superiority, but he does not make efforts to encourage the non-Luo to adopt these beliefs.[20]

---

14. Nyaga, *Impact of Witchcraft Beliefs*, 267.

15. Kgatla, *Containment of Witchcraft*, 270.

16. Van Beek, *Escalation of Witchcraft Accusations*, 301.

17. Mboya, *Paul Mboya's Luo*.

18. Mboya, *Paul Mboya's Luo*, vii.

19. Mboya, *Richo ema Kelo Chira*.

20. I use the term "superiority" here in a loose sense. Mboya's not advocating that non-Luo people follow Luo customs is an indication that the Western tendency to think that others "should" share their lifestyle is not inherent to all human communities; but arises out of the West's deeply rooted Christian history.

Melland writes in the old Africanist tradition. His attempts, almost one hundred years ago, to explain the beliefs and practices of the Kaonde tribe in Zambia portray the latter as *different* (than non-Africans).[21] In trying to help the "Bantu to advance one continually comes up against the wall called 'custom'" shares Melland, "which being considered divine is (at present) insurmountable."[22] "The dead are the real rulers of the country," adds Melland.[23] It is a "fallacy [to think that] we . . . stop witchcraft. We may flatter ourselves officially that we do, but we do not."[24] "I assert that superstition has been the chief retarding influence" to Bantu advancement, he adds.[25]

Southall realized a "problem of some profundity" in his research among the Alur (a Luo people) in East Africa: "how far my intense field experience can possibly have the same or any complementary, meaning to an African scholar."[26] To Southall, just combining western with non-western academia was not an option. They were incompatible.

Southall found that the Alur were able to convince other African ethnicities to acquiesce to Alur rule, in something akin to a colonial system of domination. He tried to find out why other tribes could acquiesce to Alur rule, but were clearly not acquiescing (at the time) to European colonial rule. "The similarity of metaphysical outlook between dominant and subject groups, which was noted

21. Melland, *In Witch Bound Africa*.

22. Ibid., 137.

23. Ibid., 149.

24. Ibid., 197.

25. Ibid., 302.

26. Southall, *Social Anthropology*, 56.

above, saved the Alur subjects from the hankering preference for independence at any price which has frustrated
African tribes even under the most enlightened European
rule" was Southall's answer.[27] So we can say that, according
to Southall, a difference between the Alur and the West has
enabled the Alur to dominate neighboring African tribal
groups relatively uncontentiously. It is common for scholars
and others to consider differences from their own peoples
to be essentially negative. Southall, however, recognized
the value of the commonality of African peoples in helping
them to work together. In other words—features of African
ways of life that Westerners may find negative could assist
in bringing an intra-African unity that is more effective
than the "unity" between European peoples and Africans.

Tempels is widely credited as having been the first
scholar to have perceived the nature of "African philosophy." Contrary to other scholars from the West, who found
Africans to be variously non-rational, to Tempels they were
acting very rationally but according to a different set of beliefs
from those held by Europeans. So "Bantu [a very widespread
African ethnicity] speak, act, live as if, for them, beings were
forces . . . ," because "being is that which has force."[28] Tempels
explains something of Bantu morality: "every act . . . which
militates against vital force or against the increase of the hi-
erarchy of the *Muntu* (person) is bad."[29] For the Bantu then—
"the worst evil—and indeed, the only real injustice—is the
harm done to the vital force . . . ."[30] As a result of his discover-

27. Southall, *Alur Society*, 234.
28. Tempels, *Bantu Philosophy*, 51.
29. Ibid., 121.
30. Ibid., 144.

ies, Tempels advocates that "the Bantu can be educated if we take as a starting point their imperishable aspiration towards the strengthening of life [i.e., vital force]" hence we shall have "found 'within' the Bantu something to render them more noble, without feeling ourselves obliged to kill first the man already existing."[31] Unfortunately, broadly speaking, we can say that Tempels's advice has not been taken and it is western education in western languages that is being imposed these days upon African nationals. I say that western languages are "imposed," because the economically dominant global powers write the equation of advantage in such a way as effectively to force so-called third world nations to use European languages in their educational systems.[32]

The final text that I want to consider, that also emphasizes difference, is by Maranz.[33] Maranz writes to help Africans and Westerners to understand one another. Maranz's research finds many similarities between Africans from different parts of the continent. So also for Westerners; "although the author recognizes that western culture can be divided into many cultures and subcultures, for the purpose of this book the term western seems justified."[34] Maranz focuses on an African "culture of sharing and of solidarity . . . [that] reflect[s] really fundamental and positive principles of African society . . . [which] are also the source of some of its greatest problems."[35] Maranz's book is a very helpful read for any Westerner

31. Ibid., 184, 171.
32. Alexander, *English Unassailable*.
33. Maranz, *African Friends*.
34. Ibid., 11.
35. Ibid., 8.

wanting to work amongst African people. It is Maranz's hope that "with better understanding of what may seem at first to be puzzling practices, Westerners will hopefully develop more understandable, comfortable, and satisfying relationships."[36]

I have classified the above texts as being those that overtly and unapologetically attempt to articulate differences between Westerners and Africans. Being written, in most cases, in western languages, they still struggle to do this effectively. Where they succeed, they end up trying to re-define English (European) terms. So Tempels considers the Bantu way of thinking to be "philosophy," when, in reality, it is very different from any known western philosophy. Maranz seems to want to re-define numerous English words in such a way that they have African meanings that are considered as legitimate as native-English ones. Evans-Pritchard and Haar take a belief that is despised in English and considered primitive and backwards (witchcraft) and explain, to an incredulous readership, that this is extant and widespread in Africa. In each of the above cases, it would seem that authors would appreciate having a distinct language that could clearly be used to describe what are distinctively African practices—something that is advocated earlier in this text (so avoiding the "polysemy" mentioned above that so troubles discourse in Africa these days).

While the above authors emphasize *difference*, there are a few who are attempting to place the emphasis on similarity. Included amongst these (according to Thiong'o—see below), are the many African novelists who have been published in English in recent decades. Chinua Achebe is

36. Ibid., 199.

one such, who rose to fame on the publishing of *Things Fall Apart* in 1958. Achebe writes: "I feel that the English language will be able to carry the weight of my African experience" (cited in Brutt-Griffler),[37] "but it will have to be a new English, still in full communion with its ancestral home but altered to suit its new African surroundings." Thiong'o is not impressed. How can it be, he asks, "that the renaissance of African authors lay in the language of Europe?"[38] Thiong'o concluded that "African literature" written in English is not "African" in the true sense at all. Rather "since the new [European] language as a means of communication was a product of and was reflecting the 'real language of life' elsewhere, it could never as spoken or written properly reflect or imitate the real life of that [African] community."[39] Instead by being forced to use English, the African ". . . was being made to stand outside himself to look at himself."[40]

One final text that I want to consider in this section is Cohen and Odhiambo's *Siaya*.[41] This was to be a break with the norm, and to be written in such a way as to be valuable and comprehensible to the "observed," i.e., the people of Siaya themselves.[42] I have discovered, through personal experience, that it is not easy to find the book entitled *Siaya* in the region of Siaya. "The epizootics that ranged between 1880 and 1900 devastated the [cattle] herds of Western

---

37. Brutt-Griffler, *World English*, vii.
38. Thiong'o, *Decolonising the Mind*, 5.
39. Ibid., 16.
40. Ibid, 17.
41. Cohen and Odhiambo, Siaya.
42. Ibid, 2–4.

Kenya" explain Cohen and Odhiambo.[43] How can that be "African thinking" I have to ask myself? It is widely known that causation in Africa is considered to be inter-personal. A massive loss of cattle by the Luo would be ascribed to some breaking of taboo, and not an "epizootic."[44] *Siaya*, undoubtedly, is written for Westerners. Even though Ogot himself praises the efforts of the writers of *Siaya* as being true to African culture,[45] it remains difficult to avoid ". . . the new invention of African societies as objects of knowledge from which these very societies are excluded."[46]

In a sense it is ironic that P'Bitek, in one way very ready to celebrate the difference between the Luo people of Uganda and White missionaries, at the same time decried the use of terms such as tribe and primitive to describe Africans.[47] It could be said that his attack on the use of English terms to describe the "other" has certainly contributed to a lot of inter-cultural fudging in more recent decades. People have been afraid that mentioning difference is implying inferiority. P'Bitek did not like it that Africans were considered by the British to be primitive. He makes his case to say—that the British (Westerners) are just as "primitive," or "more primitive" than the Africans whom they are "accusing."[48] He thereby seems to ignore the fact that it is very commonplace

43. Ibid., 75.

44. Although people perceive physical causes for events, what is important to them are the spiritual causes underlying the physical causes.

45. Ogot, *Construction of Luo Identity*, 197.

46. Ogot, *Africa*, 210.

47. P'Bitek, *African Religions*, 10, 41.

48. Ibid., 43–44.

for any people to consider others to be inferior in the ways that they are different. This certainly applies to the Luo of Kenya (closely related to P'Bitek's people) who have a term (*jamwa* pl. *mwache*) used to refer, in a derogatory way, to those who are non-Luo.

P'Bitek's pronouncements are probably widely taken as being a part of the anti-racist movement of our time. This in itself can be considered in some ways as a part of the liberal project that has grown, in part at least, out of western Christianity, and emphasizes the sanctity of the individual above all else. In this liberal philosophy, all individuals are equal, so should be treated equally—whether male, female, young, old, homosexual, heterosexual, Black or White etc. This thinking since it is rooted in the West, especially in America and Europe, takes the Euro/American man (I am intentionally using the male term here, as it is males who are setting the image that all others are expected to emulate.) as the "norm" with whom all others are to be compared. His is the standard, in so many ways, that all are to aspire to reach.

Considering all people to be equal and setting the western White male as the standard that all others are to emulate, means in effect that differences with this standard must be de-emphasized or obscured. That is; it is considered inappropriate to say that women or others, including Black men, are different in any major way to White men.

This means that the standard for "what someone ought to be" is made in America (or at least made in Europe). The image portrayed by publishing, radio and other media from those countries is that, whatever your skin color or ethnic origin, you can talk the same language, wear the same clothes, live in the same kind of house, have the same kind of hobbies, eat the same food, and even have the same mannerisms as American/European natives! This image, in the age of globalization, is transmitted around the whole world using today's ever more efficient communication media.

The people who are the source of the above "image" are also the source of donor money that Africa is becoming increasingly dependent upon. More and more of the working population in Africa is being drawn into dependence on and drawing upon the international financial and "aid" centers. The powerful people in these exchanges are the Westerners. Westerners end up making a lot of the decisions on strategy and use of resources. They (will unthinkingly) expect Africans to fit the image that they received at home of what a western man should be like. Because they *expect this*, the starting assumption of any strategy or policy is that this is the case. No programs are being instituted to bring it about—to do so would be considered racist.

In reality there are ways in which African people differ from American people. Sometimes it would be good if Africans could take on board some more American/western features: perhaps time-keeping; a work ethic; ways of thinking, and self-sufficiency. But there is no, and cannot be any, provision for such "impositions" in today's world, because to imply that such things are needed would be considered (in the West) to be racist. Instead "primitive" people are condemned to forever remain primitive.

Is difference wrong? Is it wrong to allow people to live in different ways, according to their preferences and those of their family, or people-group, or elders? Is it immoral to allow people to follow a way of life that gives them a lower life-expectancy than others? Are people free to choose the way of life they want to live?

Of course, although inadequately recognized, this is essentially a theological question. Unless we assume that there is no "god," (frankly a ridiculous assumption), the question of—who is god/God or what is god/God—is of the essence. Then also—what does God want? Unless we go back to the days when kings were considered divine; this question differs from the question "What does the president of our country want?" The answers to this question are clearly extremely consequential. If God were to announce the conditions required for people to follow in order to inherit an eternal life of joy and peace—would those conditions not be the most important for all people to follow at all times? All else would fade into insignificance by comparison; after all what are 70 years of troubled life on earth, by comparison with an eternity in paradise? Rather, as forward thinking students will work extremely hard on examinations for the sake of their future careers (sacrificing certain pleasures during examination time in anticipation of being rewarded later on) so then—what if the whole of life was like a kind of examination, set by God?

We will come back to theology in the following chapter. The main part of this chapter has focused on postulating that there are differences between African and western communities and that it will be helpful for these differences to be considered and taken into account. They should not always be ignored. Unfortunately many critical differences are invisible to the West.

5

Theology of Africa

WE HAVE already discovered that logical errors abound in the course of translation (see chapters 1 and 2). I now want to consider some issues that arise in the field of theology.

"Do African people believe in God?" was once a commonly asked question in the theological field. Mbiti did considerable research on this, and came up with the definitive answer that "Yes, indeed they do!"[1] According to Munene, for the Kikuyu; "God has full knowledge of everything, everywhere, always and from eternity, past and [present] and is therefore omniscient, omnipresent, almighty, transcendent, everlasting, holy, kind, merciful, good, and spirit."[2] It is easy to build on Munene's description and to say that, if the Kikuyu "god" (*Ng'ai*) has all these qualities, and these are considered to be qualities of God, as believed in England, then *Ng'ai* and God are the same. That is: God is *Ng'ai*. If this is the case, and the Kikuyu already know God (knew God before the missionaries came to Africa), then what does the West have to teach the Kikuyu about God? Nothing!

1. Mbiti, *African Religions*, 29.
2. Munene, *Gospel and African Belief*, 73.

71

On this basis presumably even Christians from the West, in their concern for Africa, may think they have nothing to teach about theology because the principles that need to be known about God are already known. When theological instruction is given it is generally in English—and seems to be oriented to enabling Africans (the Kikuyu in this case) to express what they already know—but in English.

Perhaps it is good to consider just how Munene came to write what she did (see direct quote above). At one time of course, the Kikuyu (and many other African people) *were* subject to a lot of missionary teaching about God. There was a time when it was thought that European Christianity was the apex of all religion and responsible for Europe's global transcendence (for example see Whitelam).[3] Missionaries from Europe and America were sufficiently enthused by their faith that they wanted to, or felt obliged to, pass it on. Originally the missionary was convinced of the need to use the language of the people.[4] Then he/she would clearly see places where Kikuyu theology was different from western theology and could try to bring about a correction.

Subsequently, however, key theological thinking for Africa (in formal circles) has been occurring using western languages. The Kikuyu themselves have begun to use western languages even when considering and describing their own contexts. For example, children in primary schools in Kenya may be asked to write what they did in the vacations using English, even though they spent their vacations in a Kikuyu village speaking only Kikuyu. Gradually English is appropriated; children (and adults) take English words as

3. Whitelam, *Invention of Ancient Israel*, 58.
4. Thiong'o, *Decolonising the Mind*, 26.

being translations of Kikuyu words and terms. For them differences between the worldview expressed in Kikuyu and the worldview expressed in English shrink. Hence they are happy to use a row of English adjectives to describe the characteristics of their God. When a native-English speaker hears from the Kikuyu about "their god," he/she is amazed (initially, but these days this has become normal) to find that the Kikuyu *Ng'ai* and the western "God" are, for almost all apparent practical purposes, identical.

The above raises further questions. It was once thought that theology was the queen of the sciences.[5] That is to say, that a people's belief about God (god) was determinative of much of their culture/beliefs and as a result, their way of life. Hence it would follow that differences in people's ways of life could be traced back to their beliefs about the "divine," and therefore, by implication, changes in people's beliefs in the divine would cause changes in people's ways of life. The linguistic assimilation described in the paragraphs above has, however, had the effect of concealing theological differences. Different people, such as Kikuyu and Westerners, may *appear* to have almost identical theology. (Theology taught in African seminaries is almost invariably western theology.) Differences in behavior, it is reasoned therefore, must have a source other than theology. Hence the relegation of theology to a level of apparent irrelevance in discussion on issues of "African development": ". . . there are solid grounds for development agencies to ignore religion in development" says Krige, although he also adds ". . . yet

5. Mars Hill Audio, *Thoughts*.

there are current trends which indicate that religion cannot be ignored."[6]

The real error is that formal discussions on African theology are engaged in English. In the few cases where formal theological instruction is given in languages other than English, it is likely to be the very basic class of people (i.e., those too uneducated to know English) who are given the content of the English syllabus in an African language. Engaging in theological debate, using African languages as used in Africa, would throw up numerous challenges—which academics these days prefer to side-step.[7] All this is connected to Africa's foreign/donor dependence, which has resulted in it being more important for people's well-being for donors to be told what they want to hear, rather than any notion of what is "true." Encouraging African development through indigenous understanding and planned change is a much more difficult route to fame and fortune. Pleasing donors and accepting their offers is a pragmatic short-cut. Unfortunately, taking this short-cut has meant that lies and deception have become very normal.[8] One can even add that since these lies and deceptions are considered normal, this discourages donors from working closely with people. But because lies and deception are not a good foundation for wealth but keep people poor, donors continue to be

---

6. Krige, *Towards a Coherent Vision*, 23.

7. An example of this in Dholuo would be the fact that two terms are used in Dholuo to translate spirit of Holy Spirit, Roho and Chuny, where chuny is anatomically the human liver.

8. Leading amongst other things to vast proportions of misuse of aid (Moyo, *Dead Aid*, 52).

active in their (futile) efforts at resolving the very poverty they are constantly causing.[9]

"Real" African theologies are more difficult for Westerners to find. They may be evident to someone who knows what they are looking for, but they are *often* not acknowledged in formal circles. It is very difficult to express them in western English, (in fact this is not only difficult—it is impossible). Efforts by Westerners at articulating African theology tend to be very hedged. Wary of the "race issue" in the West, few Europeans or Americans are ready to stick their necks out to mention unsavory truths in public fora (such as published materials). "Given the long history of interpretation and misinterpretation of Africa by non-Africans," Stinton preferred to communicate only with educated fluent English speakers, using English, yet she entitled her book *Jesus of Africa*.[10] Western authors are inclined to bend over backwards to find "positive features" in African theology. That is—to ignore translation issues and to portray African theology as much as possible as if it is European theology, but with extra attributes lost by Europeans. LeMarquand is certainly an example of this. He repeatedly praises African scholars for their practical and relevant contribution, as against North-Atlantic theologians who write primarily for "the academy."[11]

LeMarquand takes those African scholars who publish in English as having written for African audiences.[12] He does not seem to realize that to get published and to have a

9. Moyo, *Dead Aid*, 54–56.

10. Stinton, *Jesus of Africa*, 18.

11. LeMarquand, *Issue of Relevance*, 117.

12. Ibid., 114.

market for one's product, one must please Westerners and not Africans.

It is ironic that in their efforts to please and be "politically correct," theologians have been inclined to shoot themselves in the foot. When even the theologians prefer to conceal theological difference, it is no surprise that others (the African church as a whole) consider the theologians' role to be redundant. A role they seem to be left with is that of trying to take western theology in a (supposedly) African direction. LeMarquand certainly seems to be a case in point, in his praise for Africans as being relevant and practical by contrast with western scholars who only succeed in writing for the academy. Africans who realize this is happening can end up with even less respect for the western theology taught in their seminaries. Unfortunately, an alternative orthodox in-depth understanding of God, from Africa, does not seem to be available; at least not in a written form in English.

I will attempt to illustrate something more of the true state of African theology by reference to two examples. Both of them may come across as rather anti-Christian. My aim is not to deny the presence of the Christian church or the power of God in Africa, but to point out how far there still may be to go to incorporate Christian principles into African languages. A third account that illustrates what I attempt to show below would be P'Bitek although he tends to over-state his case.[13]

My first example is Evans-Pritchard's account of Zande theology (published in 1936). In this account Evans-Pritchard warns us against being too quick to assume we

13. P'Bitek, *African Religions and Religion of the Central Luo.*

know the Zande god. The Zande, he says, are ready to accept theological ideas as (long as) they do not interfere with their indigenous thought.[14] Contrary to other researchers, Evans-Pritchard has not found belief in *Mboli* ("God") to be either very prevalent or significant amongst the Azande.[15]

Below, by way of a second much more extensive example I have copied part of an article originally published in 2009:[16]

> The Kenyan Luo have other names, less frequently used in Christian circles, for God. One such is *Obong'o Nyakalaga*. *Obong'o* is given as 'only son' by Capen and Odaga - suggesting that this God is singular and unique. *Nyakalaga* refers to a force (or 'god') that 'creeps' (from the root '*lago*,' to creep). Odaga and Capen both take the term as meaning 'omnipresent'. Paul Mboya, writing at a much earlier date refers to God as 'creeping' (*lak*) within the bodies of people, reflecting the Luo belief that 'God' lives in human bodies. Contained in this seems to be a notion of God as 'life' or 'life force'. The Luo term that can be used to translate the English life, *ngima*, is much broader than its English 'equivalent' as it includes health and prosperity in general.
>
> The term *juok* (or *jok*) is often used by the Kenya Luo to translate witchcraft (*uchawi* in *Kiswahili*). Its plural (*juogi*) are the type of spirits linked with ancestors or the dead. The popular

14. Evans-Pritchard, *Zande Theology 1936*, 290.

15. Ibid, 322.

16. I have omitted the references and footnotes found in the original.

name for the witchdoctor or diviner in *Dholuo*
is *ajuoga* which implies something like 'just *juok*'
or '*juok* only'. The person-of *juok* (*jajuok*) is often
translated into English as 'night-runner' - a witch
who runs around naked at night, frightening
people by rattling windows or throwing stones
onto them or their homes. I have already mentioned that this very term *Jok* was used by the
Acholi people (a Luo tribe in Uganda) to translate 'God'. The Shilluk people consider *Juok* to be
spirit, God and body in one. Ogot has found *jok*
to be the Luo equivalent of Placide Tempels' *vital
force*, which Tempels found through his research
forms the basis for African philosophy among
the Luba people of the Congo. Tempels explains
of the African (Bantu–Luba) people that this
vital force "dominates and orientates all their
behavior."[17] The "Bantu speak, act, live as if, for
them, beings were forces," explains Tempels.[18]
Because everything, including the animal,
vegetable and mineral has 'forces', the whole of
African life is sacred - there is nowhere that *juok*
(vital force) is not found.

"The relationship between *Nyasaye* and *Juok*
is difficult to explain" writes Ocholla-Ayayo.[19]
Mboya takes *Nyasaye* and *juogi* (the plural for
juok) as synonyms in the following passage:
"*Giluongo wendo juogi; ka wendo ok wendi ionge
juogi maber. Juogi tiende Nyasaye; ok ng'ato nyalo
riembo Nyasaye; tiende, wendo ng'at Nyasaye*".[20]

17. Tempels, *Bantu Philosophy*, 21.
18. Ibid., 51.
19. Ocholla-Ayayo, *Traditional Ideology*, 219.
20. Mboya, *Luo Kitgi gi Timbegi*, 191.

This can be translated (taking "Nyasaye" as "God") as: 'Visitors are called *juogi*; so that if you do not get visitors they say that you do not have good *juogi*. *Juogi*, that means God; someone cannot chase God away, meaning that a visitor is a person of God.' (What underlies this passage seems to be the Luo people's belief that having visitors brings good fortune [*gueth* - blessing] here apparently brought by *juogi*.)

So-called 'spiritual churches' are known amongst the Luo as *Roho* churches where *Roho* (originating in Arabic and reaching *Dholuo* through *Kiswahili*) is considered to be the Holy Spirit of the Scriptures. The predecessor to *Roho* is known as having been *juogi* - the object of attention of spiritual gatherings (prior to the coming of current *Roho* practice from across the border from Uganda before 1912 and the Roho church movement in 1932). In some senses therefore *Roho* (Holy Spirit known by Christians as God as he is a member of the trinity) is a translation of *juogi*—'spirits'.

The *Dholuo* term *hawi* could be translated as 'good fortune'. Odaga, in her dictionary, goes so far as to say that *hawi* is "interchangeable with the word god." She said a similar thing in a lecture. I have frequently experienced the same in people's use of *Dholuo*. A Luo translation of goodbye is *oriti* which means something like 'he keep you' or 'he to protect you' where the 'he' presumably refers to 'god' however that 'god' may be understood. It seems almost that what 'he' (or she or it—the Luo term is gender neutral and can even refer to something inanimate) refers to is intentionally left ambiguous. An alternative farewell is '*Nyasaye obed kodi*' (God be with you), which seems to be interchangeable with '*bed gi hawi*' (be with '*hawi*'). *Jahawi* (a person of '*hawi*') is someone whose '*nyasache ber*' ('god' is good).

The Luo can refer to *Nyasache* (his/her god), often strongly implying that everyone has their own god, and that this god is like *hape* (his '*hawi*' or fortune). So it can be said that '*hape ber*' (he has good fortune), which is interchangeable with '*nyasache ber*' (his god is good). This seems to correspond in some ways to the guardian angel conception found in some Christian theology. Having 'good fortune' the Luo recognize as often arising through having a relationship with someone who is competent and is good to you. Hence explains Odaga: "your fellow human being (. . .) is your god [i.e., *nyasachi*]".[21] I have heard much the same thing said in various church circles.

One would expect the understanding of *Nyasaye* to affect the practices of churches in Luoland. If the Luo people take *Nyasaye* as being 'vital force', then one would expect churches to be seen as sources of *ngima* ('life/prosperity'). Indeed this is what is happening. This 'healing' orientation of African Christianity is known throughout the continent. (See for example Oosthuizen.) In the course of working with churches in Luoland, it has become clear to me that people are attracted to church by the prospect of material and physical reward. This can be the money and rewards carried by missionaries from western churches, and/or *hononi* ('miracles') of

---

21. Odaga, *Christianity*, 2.

various types by spirit (*Roho*) filled locals. Any Christian (or any other) movement without clear prospect of material reward (in which category I include miracles and healing) from one of these sources can get a minimal following.

Considering the above (and the many other uses of the term *Nyasaye* in Luoland) forces me to conclude that *Nyasaye* is in many ways accurately translated as the 'vital force' of Tempels; *Nyasaye* is valued according to his (her/its) manifest and immediate power. This is increasingly so, judging by the young generation's increasing attraction to Pentecostal denominations. Within Christian circles there can appear to be little *heartfelt* conception/understanding, by the Luo, of *Nyasaye* as a great High God. It is hard not to conclude that the perception of *Nyasaye* as a 'High God' could be a foreign notion brought to the Luo from the outside, and that this perception has barely penetrated many Luo people's orientation to their Christian faith.

The identity of god as life-force is evident in the Luo understanding of God. God being the power of *ngima* (life, including health and prosperity) means that *ngima* is what he is sought, in prayer, to provide. Someone who does not have *ngima* does not have God. God being the one who creeps in living bodies means that his release occurs when those living bodies are sacrificed, hence the shedding of animal blood is thought to bring blessing. The roles of a missionary and of a donor are barely distinct when the 'god' being brought is the god of prosperity. Then the success of a missionary is being defined by the material prosperity that he or she brings. I have discussed elsewhere how this role of 'provider' has the additional affect of binding the missionary force to a position of ignorance of what is 'actually going on' amongst the people they are serving.

A missionary to the Luo people is here faced with very real difficulties. The scriptures make much reference to *Nyasaye*. Thus it is made clear to the Luo people that Nyasaye of the Luo and the God of the Hebrew people, who then is identified as the Christian God in the New Testament, are one and the same. It is as if the theological task has already been completed and the missionary is left with the role of bringing *ngima* (prosperity). The God whom the people want, and the one whom they are implicitly and constantly being told that they already have, is the God who is *ngima* (life), who supplies all needs to those who worship him. Major efforts by the western donor community, both Christian and secular, to provide materially for the 'poor' in Africa further substantiate this view. The foreign missionary (and 'development') role has been captured by foundational African cosmologies and incorporated into that set of people's behaviors that seeks to fulfill ancient utopian ideals (which can barely be considered to be Christian in the orthodox sense).[22]

One factor that tends to have relegated theology out of sight to many people with an interest in Africa, is the perceived difference between spirits and god(s). That is to say—while it is widely recognized that the "belief in spir-

22. Harries, *The Name of God*, 281–285.

its" troubles African people, it is less often realized that the "study of spirits," or the study of such beliefs, is rightfully the realm of theology. The reason for this confusion, as many others have articulated in this text, can be traced to linguistic misconceptions.

Recent massive advances in communications technology have resulted in globalization advancing by leaps and bounds. Issues associated with globalization have already spawned a massive body of literature. There continues to be much debate regarding the pros and cons of globalization. Questions of globalization should not be separated from those of markets and exchanges. In other words—*I suggest there is a difference between the spread of globalization and technologies that is enabled by free-market forces, and the spread enabled by various (usually government-based) policies that act independently of markets.* Of particular interest in respect to Africa is the subsidy, often considered to be in the interests of the poor, that is putting African nations increasingly under foreign control.

To simplify what is a complex topic, one can say that western nations in particular consider one of their charitable responsibilities to be to ensure that Africa should not be left behind in the globalization process. (Underlying this is, of course, strategic self-interest, especially in the economic competition for Africa between "East" and "West.") To this end various subsidies encourage movement of facilities from the West to Africa. We have already seen how unhelpful it can be when such subsidies "force" African nations to use western languages, and western theology. Subsidy has recently been used to transplant communications technology such as the internet to Africa.[23]

One outcome of such massive spread of close links to the West, in a context in which the indigenous economy runs at a very low level, is that many are tempted to utilize the new subsidized access to the West in order to make money. Global interest in Africa, plus its reputation for poverty, provides lucrative avenues of income for an increasing proportion of the African population (at least it would seem to be so). Because "truth" was seriously compromised long ago in the African continent (see above), it is not necessarily a serious concern for recent day entrepreneurs who are seeking to take advantage of existing globalized networks.

One impact, I suggest, of the currently escalating possibilities of global communication, is that it is becoming more difficult to speak sense in formal contexts in Africa. This includes theological circles. The "truth" of Africa is being concealed under ever-expanding layers of apparent Europeanisms that miscomprehend the hurting heart of the continent. This includes Europeanisms in theology.

The only evident way to avoid the above dilemma, it seems to me, is to cease to encourage the use of European languages in Africa. The more European languages spread in today's globalized world and the more they are used in Africa, the greater the likelihood of lies, deception, and misleading untruth (or half truth). To avoid serious skewing to favor donors, and/or attack from Westerners, whether supposedly in the interests of the African continent or not, serious debate that takes account of real African contexts *must be* in African languages—even if these are out of reach

23. Kenny, *Expanding Internet.*

of most western peoples! Until this happens, serious scholarship about Africa in the globalized world is an increasing impossibility.

I believe that David Maranz has done a great favor to the world of international relations, by publishing his book *African Friends and Money Matters*.[24] He sets out therein many of the deeply troubling issues that have upset numerous western workers' attempts to work co-operatively with Africans. In essence, he outlines the way in which the patron-client system continues to be worked out in contemporary Africa. "The notion of surplus cannot (in Africa) be separated from that of selfishness," says Maranz.[25] "Borrowed money, meanwhile, is not designed to be paid off as credit is in the West," he tells us.[26] "People's social visits are always to those better off in the hope of gain," Maranz adds.[27] So Maranz goes on to articulate one shocking observation of *difference* after another.

Unfortunately Maranz does not go into any detail over the theological causes of the often counter-economical behaviors that he describes. This could be in part because Maranz realizes that some readers may be put off by any spiritual content; books that appear to be secular can get a wider readership then those that are not.

Yet underlying a lot of the behavior that Maranz describes is, I suggest, what we, in English, could call a fear of the hearts of others. This is as a result of belief that the heart of a person can have an impact that extends beyond

24. Maranz, *African Friends*.
25. Ibid., 19.
26. Ibid., 52.
27. Ibid., 76.

the observable actions of their body; in other words, to use more conventional language—fear of spirits. Perhaps a more helpful way of describing the above would be "fear of gods," where "gods" are the non-physical forces emanating from someone's heart. The English language lists some of these as: anger, frustration, hatred, disapproval, and perhaps most powerful of all, jealousy. In the African context these forces are greatly to be feared.

African visions for development often do not include doing away with the belief in these gods. Rather they advocate that the gods be placated. Such placating of gods becomes a major pre-occupation in life; a pre-occupation that is enabled these days by the provision of aid from outside the continent; a pre-occupation which reduces the efforts required for African people to look after their own wellbeing. That is—aid subsidizes the practice of African religions: in other words African gods also share in the credit for the drawing of outside aid into the continent.

Note that these "gods" are very subjective in nature. They are not up there in the sky and detached from the human community. Far from it—they are much connected to human hearts. They are very much a part of human relationships, and they determine many of the parameters of relationships. Just as an example: Western Kenyan people are renowned for their love for funerals and their fear of the sick and dying. Sick people can be almost deserted and abandoned as a result of this fear. Once the sick have died then friends and relatives crowd along to the funeral. Why is this? —a Kenya church leader was asked this question in my presence in 2009. "Because people fear being haunted," he explained. "If someone is very sick and suffering and

perhaps at risk of dying, they may well be harboring bitter-
ness or anger. The most likely people to become the targets
of such feelings are not those who stay away, whom the sick
person may not recall to memory at all. Rather, the most
likely targets of such feelings are those who are nearby, yet
fail to fully satisfy the wishes of the sick. It is therefore easy
to reason pragmatically speaking that it is better to stay
away from the seriously sick than to try and help them and
then to be haunted." (Conversation with padre of Church
of Christ in Africa, Sawagongo Parish, Gem, Kenya in
September 2009.)

This very negative impact on the care of the sick is
brought on as a result of particular beliefs in spirits/gods.
This is *bad theology*. It desperately needs correcting. It cannot be profoundly "corrected" from the outside, from a distance, or by using language that is primarily used outside of
the continent. Yet instead of people finding time to correct
such theology, the interventional strategies of outsiders
regularly (as mentioned above) encourage the continuation
of inept practices by compensating for them. In a sense that
is to say—that non-Africans have become the gods that,
through their actions, encourage the maintenance of existing African gods. This is very unlike the God of the Bible
who says:

> You shall have no other gods before me. You shall
> not make for yourself an idol in the form of any-
> thing in heaven above or on the earth beneath
> or in the waters below. You shall not bow down
> to them or worship them; for I, the LORD your
> God, am a jealous God, punishing the children
> for the sin of the fathers to the third and fourth

generation of those who hate me, but showing
love to a thousand generations of those who love
me and keep my commandments. You shall not
misuse the name of the LORD your God, for the
LORD will not hold anyone guiltless who mis-
uses his name. Remember the Sabbath day by
keeping it holy. (Exod 20:3–8, NIV)

Simiyu has a made an important observation related
to the above that deserves some attention:

"In fact, the saying that Westerners are individualistic and Africans are communal needs to be interrogated.
The prevailing culture shows in fact that Westerners are
individualistic in personal affairs and communal in their
approach to public service. Africans, on the other hand, are
individualistic in the way they approach public affairs and
communal in the way they approach personal affairs."[28]

The widely acclaimed orientation to "community" of
African people is only partly correct. In fact, the community to which they are oriented includes the dead (and not
yet born) as well as the living. This makes such use of the
English term "community" to be technically incorrect, as the
English term refers to the living (and this difference brings
considerable confusion). In other words, it is fear of spirits
of the dead (gods) and the to-be-dead that direct many of
African people's behaviors to one another, and such in turn
directs them along paths (quoting Simiyu above) that are
"individualist in the way they approach public affairs." That
is, not in the public interest, or in other words—generative
of corruption. Concern for "personal harmony with the
world" is more important than harmony of the world with

28. Simiyu, *Raising Leaders of Integrity*, 40.

God[29]—which is sought by God as classically expressed in John 3:16 (NIV) that ". . . God so loved the world that he gave his one and only son, that whoever believes in him shall not perish but have eternal life." Concern for personal gain can come as a result to be more important than the good of the community of the living as a whole.

Frankly the ways in which the personal fears of un-friendly "gods" direct certain African behaviors are unhelp-ful to African society as a whole. Supporting such things by subsidizing African communities (for example through for-eign aid) in a way that does not actively counter the people's fear of these "gods" therefore seems to be immoral. These "gods" generate poverty and various forms of suffering, and unless theological inputs are made to counter them, addi-tional "aid" brings dependence instead of advance, initia-tive, and sustainable social progress. These gods promote selfishness, individual egotism, suffering, and early death.

Maranz is careful to compare and contrast western with African ways, in a way that attempts to be impartial.[30] He points to "what Africans do," then tells us (politely it seems) that Westerners' reluctance to share in what is hap-pening arises because "they do not want to further con-tribute to waste and failure."[31] This has many implications. Westerners tend to be compassionate from a distance, but can be horrified by what they see happening among African communities when they draw near. Such "horror" forces the African into denial, which when the Westerner has withdrawn from the African context, no-one can refute

29. Chike, *Proudly African*, 236.

30. Maranz, *African Friends*.

31. Ibid., 104.

intelligently any longer. In other words, elements of African life, including "theological evil," continue because the current approaches of the West to Africa make it impossible for these elements to be resolved (see Douglas for more on this).[32]

Weber's renowned thesis on the protestant work ethic can helpfully be brought to our attention here. "One of the fundamental elements of the spirit of modern capitalism, and not only of that but of all modern culture: rational conduct on the basis of the idea of the calling, was born . . . from the spirit of Christian asceticism" wrote Weber.[33] The impact of "Christian asceticism" is profoundly evident, according to Weber, in having set the whole course of western life. Yet its reality in contemporary times is denied. This is like someone rescued from drowning at sea who, once back on dry land, denies that he has ever seen the need for a lifeboat, and dismantles the lifeboat industry—thus denying others the benefit of the salvation that he/she has enjoyed. That is—the selfishness of the West today that denies the role of God in his relationship with the poor, leaves people in Africa stranded "out at sea"; or as Ha-Joong puts it in the title of his book, the West is "kicking away the ladder" so as to prevent others from using it.[34]

That is to say—it appears that missionaries to Africa may have "erred, theologically, in not understanding the gospel in the way that the apostle Paul did," and that this error could have come from their over-blind following

32. Douglas, *Sorcery Accusations Unleashed*, 190–191.

33. Weber, *Protestant Ethic*, 180.

34. Ha-Joong, *Kicking away the Ladder*.

of examples set by secular bodies.[35] Few would deny that "It is better to teach a man to fish than to give him a fish." Too few have realized that it is the gods/spirits/powers of Africa who are cutting open the fishing net and allowing the fish to escape, and that it is the almighty God who can intervene and enable African people to fish for themselves. Perhaps in saying this, I have lost what might have been my secular readership. Yet I have to conclude it is better that I have fewer readers and I tell the truth, than many readers to whom I tell a half-truth.

As intimated above—missionaries who have been taking a message of God's love to Africa should not be too quick to pat themselves on the back. A message given may not be the same as the message received. The latter can only be known by the receiving end, but western missionaries have kept themselves too distant from the receiving end to know what is really going on there. Hence—another reason for the following of the principle of vulnerable mission; hence—the need for some western missionaries to operate in their ministries using local language and resources (and so become sensitive to the outlook and need of the African people whom they are seeking to reach).

It is not the number of mission personnel that is of primary importance, nor the size of their projects, number of the churches they have planted etc. Christians are the "salt of the earth" (Matt 5:13), and it is their saltiness that counts, and can radically improve the flavor of the whole meal (the whole of life).

Theologians, as others, have not realized the deceptiveness of the use of western languages in Africa. In their use

35. Bediako, *Their Past*, 6.

polysemy results in the Westerner understanding one thing but the African another. That is a *very* poor way to work with the gospel of Jesus Christ. Unfortunately the African people's own stated linguistic preferences for European languages cannot be taken at face value. They often have no choice. Western languages are financially loaded way above and beyond the competition. The African person being faced with the choices: "Western language, and ignorance, and wealth" or "African language plus understanding and poverty" will prefer the former. The promotion of western languages, using diverse types of foreign subsidy (hidden or unhidden), has been one of the most immoral acts of the international community in Africa—and this continues to have devastating effects. Misleading assumptions, such as that God is the same as *Ngayi/Lesa/Nyasaye* etc. have arisen as a result of the kind of logical errors mentioned above.

Development has been described by Ogot as ". . . a sacred cow which cannot be offended or questioned."[36] That is, models of "development" for the third world have been taken as if these models should never be challenged. A truly self-critical reflection on the part of advocates of development has been rendered almost impossible by their own initial setting of its parameters. "Development plans" for Africa have been designed by the West for implementation in Africa and once again their design has been in western languages. They seem to ignore god/God's role in people's lives, which Krige says ". . . is to ignore the main driving force of many of the poorest people in the world."[37]

36. Ogot, *Building on the Indigenous*, 140.
37. Krige, *Towards a Coherent Vision*, 23.

As in the past, so today, people's fear of spirits (gods) and witchcraft can be overcome through faith in God. Such faith can be taught by those who have it and are prepared to live it in a way that brings them alongside African people linguistically and economically.

Note that my criticisms of secular practices (such as development, aid, and subsidies) do not necessarily mean that I consider that all of them should cease immediately. On the contrary—they may need re-evaluating, and my hunch is that many present-day practices really should not continue. Taken alone they resemble food without salt— worthy of spitting out. If they allow some salt to be added, perhaps something can be rescued. I don't know; I am open to that option, but for now let's work on the salt and take away the hegemony from the materialist-development fraternity, a hegemony that rightfully belongs to God.

6

Conclusion and "Vulnerable Mission in Practice"

THIS CHAPTER further expands on the practical conclusion, for which prior chapters have sought to give a reason. First I will point out how the content of the prior chapters all point to the importance of the two principles of vulnerable mission (VM). That is: that some western missionaries to Africa carry out their key ministries using local languages and local resources. I will then articulate in more detail practical ways in which VM principles can be followed in practice.

The first chapter looked at the deception inherent in present day assumptions regarding inter-cultural communication and understanding. Incredibly we found that what is foreign (African) is so domesticated for consumption by western audiences, as to be purified of its foreignness (Africanness). The West thinks that it is hearing from and communicating with the rest of the world, when it can more accurately be said to be pre-occupied with looking at its own reflection in a distorted mirror. This was illustrated by comparing different cultures to different sports, by drawing on recent discoveries in language pragmatics, and by looking at translation as a process of misguided logic.

In every case outlined in the above paragraph, it became clear that it is far from sufficient to work with a people in any other than their own language. If not in their mother tongue, communication with them should be done in a language closely related to their own (such as *Kiswahili* in East Africa). Or, in the case of the Westerner working outside of the West, even the use of another European language (that one learns from the people one is trying to reach) is better than the use of one's mother tongue (e.g., English) in communication with them. (This is because a European language learned in situ will be learned according to the way local people use it. This remains a long way short however of the ideal we are here promoting—using an African language to communicate with African people.) In order to acquire a close understanding, and to relate to people on a spiritual level, with a message about God in an honest and open way, the use of their language learned from them is an *enormous* head-start.

The second chapter considers the writings of other linguists as they pertain to this issue. Brock-Utne leads a campaign in favor of African languages. Brutt-Griffler has pointed out that colonialists realized the damage that could be done by the internationalization of English well over fifty years ago. Pennycock and Rassool drive home the vital importance of mother-tongue use in education. Sperber and Wilson demonstrate graphically that communication is about context, and in a sense only assisted by words—making the perceptive reader fully aware that to merely translate "words," according to some notion of their "meaning," can be totally missing the point of communication. Blommaert and Verschueren apply such thinking to a research project on immigrants in Belgium—and find that knowledge of obscured conversations is essential as background to enable accurate understanding of public discourse concerning Muslim immigrants in Belgium. Drawing further on Steiner and Leech—the chapter makes a clear case in favor of encouraging African nations to run their affairs using indigenous languages.

A further reason for advocating that some missionaries operate their key ministries using indigenous languages is to enable them to contribute to and learn from what is actually happening on the continent. By using indigenous languages, they will be encouraging Africans, who have been "brought up" by neo-colonial powers, to believe that there can be a future for the continent and for their people other than as protégés of Westerners.[1] This gives hope for the gospel of Jesus Christ—currently all too closely tied in with modernizing and westernizing ideals. A missionary who so operates will become both astute in listening to the heartbeat of the people being reached and will reach them at a depth way beyond the formal discourses going on. Following discourse in the vernacular will enable a learning of the "state of the nation" as it is, and not only as Westerners prefer to have it portrayed. Such insights can be of critical importance in enabling a missionary to contribute intelligently to God's plan for the future of a people.

The sacred cows of development and foreign aid are discussed in chapter 3.[2] The peculiar orientation by the West today, with regard to the rest of the people on the globe, is seen to be rooted in implicit faith in historical materialism. While there is truth in that doctrine, it is clearly not the whole truth. Hence the maladies and distortions caused by

1. Tshehla, *Can Anything Good*, 19.
2. Ogot, *Building on the Indigenous*, 140.

the development fraternity; a fraternity which is neverthe-
less largely self-perpetuating due to invested financial interests. "Development thinking" is imposed by those with
a financial surplus, and is a version of colonialism without
responsibility.

Many Christians in the West have come to see aid to
the poor in the third world as a substitute for sacrifices for
propitiating sins, or more specifically, for relieving guilt.
This, combined with belief in historical materialism, has
been shown (by authors such as Grigg and Martin) to have
produced a very strong tension in thinking about mission
and the relationship of the wealthy West to the suffering in
the poor countries of the world. These authors' insistence
on generosity clashes constantly (incredibly) with western
people's realization of the damage often done by their generosity to the poor.

For some reason, perhaps surprisingly, not one of the
authors familiar with this matter has addressed the "simple"
solution to this dilemma as put forward by the Alliance for
Vulnerable Mission (AVM; see www.vulnerablemission.
org). This solution is—that *some* western missionaries by-
pass donor roles when it comes to their key ministry. They
need not feel guilty about doing so, because the money they
are giving away is someone else's anyway (in the case of supported western missionaries) and the total amount to be
given to the poor need not be reduced. They resemble Jesus,
in that, to further his ministry, he also frequently refused to
call on the resources he had available, preferring instead to
promote ministry in a way that his disciples would be able
to continue after his departure.

The following chapter looked at "What is Africa?" It
found that perceptions of Africa held in the West could not

be accurate, because even the languages that make up the building blocks of African life are a mystery to the vast majority of Westerners. Many authors have written to articulate *difference* in Africa, such as Haar, Southall, Tempels, Maranz—but the West does not really know how to respond to such differences. The case made by others that "Africa is not different" is shown to be faulty. Implicit western insistence that the White western male must be the model for all others to aspire to, and indeed that others can and have reached their aspirations, is shown as both misguided and harmful. This is because, if differences are assumed not-to-be-there in the globalized world, planning is ineffective because it ignores the truth, and those who would attempt to close-the-gap between peoples are not permitted to do so, because technically if there is no *difference* there is no gap.

These assumptions regarding sameness are blinding and distorting the true missionary and "development" task. They are perpetuated in the case of an individual Westerner primarily in two ways:

1. Use of a non-native language that precludes the Westerner from acquiring "correct" insights;

2. The Westerner's financial power that makes him or her into a pawn in power-games that can render "normal," honest, uninterested relationships with nationals almost impossible.[3] The way to counter these is exactly what is advocated in VM—only to use local languages and local resources in one's ministry.

The fifth chapter noticed how the tendency by Westerners, to use English and "western theology" in their teaching in Africa, can make the very issues they should be

3. "Uninterested" in the sense of the African patron/client system.

addressing disappear from view. As a result of this, theology becomes a means of access to western resources that is otherwise largely irrelevant. Such "shooting of itself in the foot" by theology is one of the most incredible and least recognized themes being played out in Africa today. Of course, it does not prevent God from working, but it has brought a mismatch between God's working and theological teaching. The failure by God's servants (and I address Westerners) to follow biblical precedent in mission by cocooning themselves in languages and resources foreign to Africa, even while serving in Africa, has enabled pernicious African spirits to continue much of their destructive work out of sight of that which should have muted them.

Our consideration of theology brings the advantages of VM into sharp focus, because the theologian deals with matters of the heart, matters of profound interpersonal relationship, of hope, love, of the future and of eternity. All these are deeply cultural, and necessary as the foundation for building any of the dreams of "development" planners. Even in places where non-theologians may (perhaps) get away with ignoring the VM principles, they are much more the bread and butter of the bible teacher, pastor, evangelist, overseer, priest, and prophet. If Westerners do not engage in VM they can in effect be doing very little but spouting what is foreign, and leaving the difficult work of translating the gospel to nationals. That is a misleading impact and disappointing misappropriation of the resources of faith and godly gifts that many Westerners possess.

We are left with our final concern—how can VM be implemented in practice? A related question we can ask is: How should our practical implementation of VM be further guided by the insights we have acquired through our reading of this book?

Like all simple principles, the outworking of VM is bound to get complex. Throughout this discussion, however, let us not lose sight of the simplicity. What is being advocated is simply that some western missionaries need to engage their ministries using the languages and resources of the localities they are in when working outside of the West.

Some could take VM as being an attack on conventional mission's practice by the West. Fundamentally it should not be and need not be. It may be perceived as such by "conventional" missionaries because it reveals weaknesses in their approach to ministry. This should not be threatening to someone who is convinced that they are correct in the way they are serving the Lord. It should only be truly threatening to those who are concerned that weak spots in their ministry may be exposed. VM asks those who do their ministry with money and in foreign languages to give up their claim to hegemony. Those who work on the basis of moral imperatives; "we must do x, y, z because we can . . ." can feel threatened by VM because it rejects many of the moral imperatives of historical materialistic thinking.[4]

A VM may have to create and then maintain a distance with a conventional missionary while working with

4. Much justification for action by Westerners in Africa is on the basis of the "moral imperative" that says that not doing good when one has the possibility to do so is in effect "sin." The "moral imperative" is further based on notions of equality—that if the West has more of something or a better version of something than those outside of the West that there is a moral imperative to equalize access to that product—whatever it is.

the same people. This is simply because a VM's close association with someone involved in generous giving can quickly have "the poor" suspect that he/she is influencing their colleague's decisions regarding allocation of funds. This is tantamount to VMs having resources to give out themselves, which is contrary to their way of working. This is, of course, the same issue that faces many non-western nationals; if they associate closely with a wealthy missionary, others will think that they are in it for the money, that they are benefiting and that they are influencing the way the donor is using their funds.

In parallel with the above paragraph, it is important to say that a VM is not a "spy" working on behalf of a mission agency or project. A close understanding of the local context and people can give a VM insider knowledge regarding the activities of other western mission activities in their area. They may perceive, for example, that a certain church leader who is working under a missionary/donor colleague has taken a second wife without the missionary's knowledge. Or they can be party to information about certain corrupt deeds and activities going on in relation to a fellow missionary's project. The VM must remain silent in such circumstances. Not to do so would mean becoming the enemy of the people who are benefiting from the ignorance of the donor concerned. (In many contexts, the position of the VM is much like that of nationals—who may also remain silent on such issues.)

To some, the above may be a difficult moral issue. It is a moral dilemma constantly faced by African nationals that arises from the kinds of mission and development practices critiqued in this book. It is one contribution to the rising levels of corruption in Africa; people can be obliged to tell lies, until the telling of lies comes to be considered no longer morally wrong.

A VM must be ready to move between two lifestyles, and to accept both (essentially) as they are. This is not always easy. So when a VM mixes with western colleagues he/she must accept them for who they are. One community a VM lives with may be so poor as to rejoice if they get $1.00 as it may buy a meal for a whole family. Another community VM spends time with may happily spend $20.00 for a meal for just one person. Telling the poor how the other half lives, will introduce tensions of jealousy. Suggesting to the wealthy that they are being over-extravagant will result, in due course, in one's being rejected by them. A VM should not use their privileged access to one group in their relationships with another. They are not amongst the poor to tell them of the West, nor amongst the West to tell them of the poor. Rather, on both sides—they are there to witness for Jesus Christ.

This separation of roles is vital. A geographical separation may be a helpful part of it. In one place a VM can be imitating the behavior of the poor (in terms of language, etc.) and in another the behavior of Westerners. This dual identity should not be a secret. There should be some exchange between the two communities for the sake of accountability. For example, the non-Westerners that a VM mixes with need to know that the VM continues to live an upright life even when amongst western colleagues, and vice versa.

A VM also needs a western context in which to blow off steam. That is, a place to freely discuss the challenges being faced without fear of rejection or of evoking defensive responses by western colleagues. This means that a VM needs to have missionary colleagues (Westerners), who may not be VMs themselves; but who are there to support someone practising VM. I suggest, as does Grigg, that this could be an older couple, and that perhaps one day per week can be taken in interacting with this couple.[5] It will be advantageous if a VM can also meet with other VMs so as to share and compare experiences.

This older couple will need to be prepared to cope with the clash of cultural realities they receive from the VM. Ideally—they will have had mission experience or, even better, VM experience, so that they understand the kinds of issues that the VMs in their care may face. The primary role of this couple is not to interact with nationals, but with western VMs who are working with nationals.

The back-up support for VMs is not really there to advise them, although to an extent they must give advice, reflection, counsel etc. from what they hear. The advice the supporters can give includes encouraging the VMs to:

1. Keep to the two VM principles even when under pressure to deviate from them;

2. Teach the Bible and follow its teachings in all their diversity and depth.

VM is about bridging a gap, and reaching people where they are. Therefore it is about taking difference seriously, rather than ignoring it and hoping it will go away. "Mission"

5. Grigg, *Companion to the Poor*, 205. I acknowledge that in practice it may be difficult to find such willing and available "older couples."

in Africa has often been done by drawing local people to a mission station where they have met the gospel along with the western culture of the missionaries. VM is about having a "mission station" that is a base for missionaries to retreat to, but for the missionaries to minister beyond the boundaries of the station: geographically, economically, culturally, and linguistically.

VMs will differ in how much of their lives they will contribute to "ministry" and how much they will spend within their western circle. Couples will probably be more tied to the western context than singles. It is feasible that a missionary may spend only one day per week doing VM and the other six at the station. Obviously the more time one can give the better—the more effectively one will learn language, etc.; but the key of VM is not that one has to spend all one's time in ministry. One important aspect of VM is to make a clear demarcation between the ministry context in which they use local languages and resources, and the missionary's "western" context.

Some mixing of the two can occur. Talking in indigenous languages need not be banned at the western station, and work issues to do with the West at the ministry site. The key consideration could be looked at as being that:

1. The mission not become a place for acquiring financial or material gain or knowledge of foreign languages on the part of nationals;

2. The ministry site should not become over affected by whatever outside inputs are to be found at the mission.

VM is not advocating a "simple lifestyle" as such. In many ways, it is only indirectly concerned with the "lifestyle" of the missionary. Its concern is with ministry. If a missionary wants to live in a mansion and eat ice-cream while sitting watching movies on the internet—that, as far as VM is concerned, is their business. But, that must not be the context in which the missionary meets the nationals with whom they are to minister. Frankly, it is helpful for ministry for a missionary to lead a "simple lifestyle," and for that lifestyle to be as close as possible to that of the people being reached. But, the decision on lifestyle is left to the missionary. This should avoid the intrusiveness that arises when church or mission attempt to dictate missionary eating habits, house size, television viewing habits, etc.

In taking the above stand, VM is opposing those who would respond to jealousy. Classically, it is thought that Africans will get jealous if a missionary lives at a very much higher standard than they. So indeed they might; but jealousy is a sin. It is not something to be encouraged, or something to be feared.

Some may ask about the relationship between VM and marriage and family. In short, a VM will seek to keep and then to bring up a family primarily in one culture. So then, an American missionary couple will bring up their children as Americans. At the same time, the parents or a parent will take time out to engage in ministry *away from the family home*. A typical arrangement may be that the father of the family be absent and engaged in ministry for two or three days weekly. During that time he should sleep away and have minimal contact with home. Those with whom he is involved in ministry will also have minimal contact with his wife and children.

It should be added here that, at least from my personal experience, people are very understanding of foreigners' needs for ongoing contact with their own people and their own people's way of doing things. I do not think that any-one in a UK church set up would object if a Chinese person who assists in the running of the church, also spent two days per week at home living in a Chinese way with his/her family. Neither would they be upset if the Chinese person preferred Chinese food, or even if they were oriented to the use of Chinese medicine. People may become concerned if the Chinese person took it upon himself to try to convince Brits of the superiority of Chinese ways, or to force them to eat Chinese food in the name of Christ. In the same way in Africa: African people have no cause to object to their mis-sionary maintaining a western way of life, providing that they do not then imply that their way is superior, or attempt to force their lifestyle or language onto the African people in the name of the gospel.

VM is a way of taking the impact of one's context on one's understanding of the gospel seriously. A VM takes the Bible as seriously as any other Christian, and is guided by it. In terms of ministry amongst the people of a non-western culture, VMs will want to understand the Bible in the way that nationals of that culture do so. An orientation to VM is not a doing away with other missiological advice. It is taking it on board, and advocating that the best way to implement it is by having some missionaries follow VM principles.

I believe that VM could work, and could be helpful, for a variety of mission-sending set-ups. Large mission agencies or sending churches would have to make some changes in their operations, philosophy, and missionary attitude. Commitment to local languages and their working without access to outside resources means both that a VM may turn up relatively few quantifiable results,[6] and will be relatively unavailable for administrative tasks. A mission team who expects every team-member to contribute to their corporate well-being may be disappointed in a VM. Because a VM seeks to minister in the way a local would minister, VMs are likely to draw on the services of their colleagues with little to offer in return (as tends to be the case with nationals in mission to Africa today). (Mission efforts in Africa tend to be run by Westerners, with non-western nationals as beneficiaries.) Any missionaries who do not appreciate VM strategy could consider a VM to be a parasite, not contributing to the mission effort as a whole, but instead as diluting the impact of resources that are intended "for Africans"! For example, a VM will use the medical services of his mission like anyone else, but has nothing comparable to offer to the missionary doctor or his family. It seems that for a VM to "succeed," fellow missionaries must be ready to "serve him (her)," as they do nationals.

A wise missionary who does not follow VM practices will realize that assistance given to a VM in time of need, is a way of demonstrating Christian love, perhaps even more effectively than such assistance that is offered to a national. It should become a part of the "ministry to the poor" of a VM's missionary colleagues! This may be difficult to achieve in practice. It has been my personal experience that many western missionaries coming to Africa tend to "fight"

6. I mention this in the light of the requirement often advocated these days for ministry results to be in some way quantifiable, often for purposes of being accountable.

with fellow missionaries rather than "serve" them. They see themselves as coming to serve Africans, and often do not want a fellow Westerner to get in the way of this service. They want to listen to the African! They may not be overly-impressed if told that actually they cannot understand the African, and should instead listen to a VM. This will require an extra dose of humility on the part of the wider missions' force.

I have already explained that a VM often cannot relate too closely to other missionaries working among the same people. Then why and how can I say that a conventional missionary should listen to VMs (as above)? VMs should not force themselves into close contact with other field missionaries or projects if they are not made welcome. Relationships with fellow western missionaries may be strained if the latter feel "threatened" by the vulnerable approach. Because of this, a VM may have little opportunity to feed back what they learn to western colleagues in the field. In such a case they need to find someone else to whom they can relate their experiences—whether in the field or in a "sending" country. VMs should be feeding back into the hierarchies of mission organizations. They should be listened to by designers of mission strategy, and thus their advice should be filtering through even to those missionaries who are not VMs. The reasons for this are explained in prior chapters in this text—the VM is uniquely positioned to communicate the truth on the ground back to the "bosses" in the West; more so than the African national because the VM understands the West, and more so than other missionary colleagues, because he/she understands Africa.

Having said the above, it is also important to say that a VM must be ready to face criticism from missionary colleagues, and/or from nationals. Vulnerability is indeed vulnerability. We can be vulnerable because we are invulnerable.[7] VMs should be very slow to buy themselves out of trouble. If they do suffer undue criticism or unkindness from missionary colleagues, they should be ready to take it—and just to keep in mind the objective of continuing to serve despite and through whatever form that relationship takes. They need to be slow to "put their foot down" and insist on changes. They should be ready to be "used as a doormat." They ought to be ready to see things change slowly, and to persist regardless of tribulation, whatever form it may take. Of course they should listen carefully to their detractors so as not to fail to understand and to respond to valid critiques. I have already pointed out above—that they are not there to tell other missionaries that they are "wrong." They should consider others better than themselves (Phil 2:3).

VM is about the power of powerlessness. That is—the use of unconventional (especially godly) avenues of power. Direct and evident sources of power that VMs prefer to avoid include friends in government, financial resources, use of "powerful languages," use of the courts, and so on. A VM's power is to be seen in their determination to continue the course despite all opposition. Surely people will marvel if they see a Westerner who has left the assumed "comforts" of their own people's way of life to serve diligently for decades whether or not "results" in the traditional sense of the word (statistical etc.) are forthcoming. I believe that this is a model that Jesus showed us. He also refused to seek

7. Laura, *I Can Be Vulnerable*.

friendships with powerful people as a means to advance his ministry. This is well illustrated by his blunt response to Nicodemus's question in the Gospel written by John (3:2–3). We see little or no evidence of his having protected himself or made inroads into the political fraternity by acquiring privileged access to the powerful.

I have talked a great deal about missionaries, assuming that the primary aim of outside intervention is to spread the gospel of Jesus Christ. But I take much of the content of this text to be equally relevant to those endeavoring to encourage "development" in Africa, as defined in different ways. I do believe (unlike Prah cited above) that the ultimate means of promoting development is through sharing Christ. I encourage readers to explore this hypothesis further by looking at other writings at www.vulnerablemission.org.

My intention in this book, as in other activities engaged by the AVM is to address the "West." I am not attempting to "tell Africans what to do," or even Koreans, or other missionaries of non-western origin. Should they be helped by reading some of this material, then I am more than glad. Those who would make efforts (often consisting of scholarships and subsidies) to draw non-Westerners into western debates such as these can unfortunately swamp "indigenous debates" that should be going on, as well as distorting the intra-western discussion. This book is addressed to Westerners, especially native-English speakers, and others need to realize that they are "over-hearers," with all that this implies.

I have looked at writings by Martin and Grigg and other missions' scholars. My intention in considering them in this text has been to critique them through a VM lens.

This is not to say that they do not have a lot of very important and helpful points to make. VM does not represent an over-turning of prior missiological wisdom. Rather, it represents an enabling to do that to which others aspire, but all too often fail to achieve. A major reason they fail to "achieve," I believe, is their taking insufficient cognizance of the importance of the use of indigenous languages and resources in Christian ministry outside of the West.

Bibliography

Achebe, Chinua. *Things Fall Apart.* Nairobi: Heinemann, 1958.

Açıkgöz, Fırat, and Olcay Sert. "Interlingual Machine Translation: Prospects and Setbacks", 2006. Online: http://www.eric.ed.gov /PDFS/ED495835.pdf.

Akrong, Abraham. "A Phenomenology of Witchcraft in Ghana." In *Imagining Evil: Witchcraft beliefs and accusations in contemporary Africa,* edited by Gerrie Ter Haar, 53–66. Trenton, NJ: Africa World Press, 2007.

Alexander, Neville. "English Unassailable but Unattainable: The dilemma of language policy in South African education." Paper presented at the Biennial Conference of the International Federation for the Teaching of English, University of Warwick, England, UK, July 7–10, 1999. Online: http://eric.ed.gov/PDFS /ED444151.pdf.

Bediako, Kwame. "Their Past is also our Present. Why all Christians have need of ancestors: Making a case for Africa." *African Institute for Contemporary Mission and Research Bulletin* 6 (2007) 1–16.

Benhabib, Seyla. *The Rights of Others: Aliens, residents and citizens.* Cambridge: Cambridge University Press, 2004.

Blommaert, Jan, and Jef Verschueren. *Debating Diversity: Analysing the discourse of tolerance.* London: Routledge, 1998.

Blount, B. G. "The Luo of South Nyanza, Western Kenya." In *Cultural Source Materials for Population Planning in East Africa.* Vol. 2, edited by Angela Molnos, 275–80. Nairobi: East African Publishing House, 1972.

Bongmba, Elias K. "Witchcraft and the Christian Church: Ethical Implications." In *Imagining Evil: Witchcraft beliefs and accusations in contemporary Africa,* edited by Gerrie Ter Haar, 113–42. Trenton, NJ: Africa World Press, 2007.

Brock-Utne, Birgit, et al. *Language of Instruction in Tanzania and South Africa (LOITASA)*. Dar-es-Salaam: E and D, 2003.

Brutt-Griffler, Janina. *World English: A study of its development*. Bristol: Multilingual Matters, 2002.

Chesos, Richard, "Walimu Wasiokuwa na Diploma Kufutwa," *Taifa Leo*, February 21, 2005.

Chike, Chiger. "Proudly African, Proudly Christian: The Roots of Christologies in African Worldview." *Black Theology: An International Journal*. 6 (2008) 221–40.

Cohen, David William, and E. S. Atieno Odhiambo,. *Siaya: The historical anthropology of an African landscape*. London: James Currey, 1989.

Crystal, David. *English as a Global Language*. Cambridge: Cambridge University Press, 1997.

Danfulani, Umar Habila Dadem. "Anger as a Metaphor for Witchcraft; the relation between Magic, Witchcraft and Divination among the Mupun of Nigeria." In *Imagining Evil: Witchcraft beliefs and accusations in contemporary Africa*, edited by Gerrie Ter Haar, 143–82. Trenton, NJ: Africa World Press, 2007.

Desai, Zubeida. "A Case for Mother Tongue Education?" In *Language of Instruction in Tanzania and South Africa (LOITASA)*, edited by Birgit Brock-Utne et al., 45–68. Dar-es-Salaam: E and D, 2003.

Douglas, Mary. "Sorcery Accusations Unleashed: The Lele revisited, 1987." *Africa: Journal of the International African Institute* 69 (1999) 177–93. Online: http://jstor.org/pss/1161021.

Dovlo, Elom. "Witchcraft in Contemporary Ghana." In *Imagining Evil: Witchcraft beliefs and accusations in contemporary Africa*, edited by Gerrie Ter Haar, 67–92. Trenton, NJ: Africa World Press, 2007.

Ellis, Stephen. "Witching-times: A theme in the histories of Africa and Europe." In *Imagining Evil: Witchcraft beliefs and accusations in contemporary Africa*, edited by Gerrie Ter Haar, 31–52. Trenton, NJ: Africa World Press, 2007.

Evans-Pritchard, E. E. "Zande Theology." *Sudan Notes and Record* 19 (1936) 5–46.

———. "Zande Theology 1936." In *Social Anthropology and Other Essays*, 288–329. New York: Free Press, 1966.

————. *Witchcraft, Oracles and Magic among the Azande.* (Abridged.) Oxford: Clarendon Press, 1976.

Foster, G. M. *Traditional Societies and Technological Change.* 2nd ed. London: Harper and Row, 1973.

Grigg, Viv. *Companion to the Poor: Christ in the urban slums.* Revised Edition. Milton Keynes: Authentic Media, 2004.

Haar, Gerrie Ter, ed. *Imagining Evil: Witchcraft beliefs and accusations in contemporary Africa.* Trenton, NJ: Africa World Press, 2007.

Ha-Joong, Chang. *Kicking Away the Ladder: Development strategy in historical perspective.* London: Anthem Press, 2002.

Harries, Jim. "Good by Default and Evil in Africa." *Missiology: an international review,* 34 (2006) 151–64.

————, 2007a. "Difficulties in Giving: What to give, how to give, why to give, who to give, when to give, if to give?" Online: http://www.jim-mission.org.uk/articles/difficulties-in-giving.html (accessed May 6, 2009).

————, 2007b. "Pragmatic Theory Applied to Christian Mission in Africa: With Special Reference To Luo Responses To 'Bad' in Gem, Kenya." PhD thesis, University of Birmingham, 2007. Online: http://etheses.bham.ac.uk/15/ (accessed January 2, 2010).

————. "The Name of God in Africa and Related Contemporary Theological, Development and Linguistic Concerns." *Exchange: Journal of Missiological and Ecumenical Research* 38 (2009) 271–91.

Hinfelaar, Hugo F. "Witch-hunting in Zambia and the International Illegal Trade." In *Imagining Evil: Witchcraft beliefs and accusations in contemporary Africa,* edited by Gerrie Ter Haar, 229–46. Trenton, NJ: Africa World Press, 2007.

Kenny, Charles J. "Expanding Internet Access to The Rural Poor in Africa." Online: http://www.itu.int/africainternet2000/Documents/doc7_e.htm.

Kgatla, Selaelo Thias. "Containment of Witchcraft Accusations in South Africa: A search for transformational approach to curb the problem." In *Imagining Evil: Witchcraft beliefs and accusations in contemporary Africa,* edited by Gerrie Ter Haar, 269–92. Trenton, NJ: Africa World Press, 2007.

Krige, Skip. "Towards a Coherent Vision for Faith-Based Development." *Journal for Theology for Southern Africa* 132 (2008) 16–37.

Laura H. 2009. "I Can Be Vulnerable Because I Am Invulnerable!" Online: http://anearnestconsideration.blogspot.com/2009/10/i-can -be-vulnerable-because-i-am.html.

LeMarquand, Grant. *An Issue of Relevance: A comparative study of the story of the bleeding woman (Mk. 5:25–34, Mt. 9:20–22, Lk. 8:43–48) in North Atlantic and African Contexts.* Oxford: Peter Lang, 2004.

Leech, Geoffrey H. *Principles of Pragmatics.* London and New York: Longman, 1983.

Malekela, George A. "English As a Medium of Instruction In Post-Primary Education In Tanzania: Is it a fair policy to the learners?" In *Language of Instruction in Tanzania and South Africa (LOITASA),* edited by Birgit Brock-Utne et al., 102–12. Dar-es-Salaam: E and D, 2003.

Maranz, David. *African Friends and Money Matters: observations from Africa.* Dallas: SIL International, 2001.

Mars Hill Audio, 2006. "Thoughts on the Queen of the Sciences." Online: http://www.marshillaudio.org/resources/article.asp?id=127.

Martin, Jonathan. *Giving Wisely?: Killing with kindness or empowering lasting transformation.* Oregon: Last Chapter Publishing, 2008.

Mbambo, Samuel Kareto. "The Mbambi Brought the Message: shitera, witchcraft of revenge." In *Imagining Evil: Witchcraft beliefs and accusations in contemporary Africa,* edited by Gerrie Ter Haar, 185–204. Trenton, NJ: Africa World Press, 2007.

Mbiti, John S. *African Religions and Philosophy.* London: Heinemann, 1969.

Mboya, Paul. *Richo ema Kelo Chira.* Nairobi: East African Publishing House, 1978.

———. *Luo Kitgi gi Timbegi.* Kisumu: Anyange Press, 1983.

———. *Paul Mboya's Luo Kitgi gi Timbegi.* Translated by Jane Achieng. Nairobi: Atai Joint, 2001.

McKay, Sandra Lee. *Teaching English as an International Language: Rethinking goals and approaches.* Oxford: Oxford University Press, 2002.

Melland, F. H. *In Witch Bound Africa: An account of the primitive Kaonde Tribe and their beliefs.* Philadelphia: J.B.Lippincott Company, 1923.

Meerkoller, Dirk. "Markets, Language in Education and Societies Economic Stratification." In *Language of Instruction in Tanzania and South Africa (LOITASA)*, edited by Birgit Brock-Utne et al., 35–44. Dar-es-Salaam: E and D, 2003.

Moyo, Dambisa. *Dead Aid: Why aid is not working and how there is another way for Africa.* London: Allen Lane, Penguin Books, 2009.

Moyo, Dambisa, and Jacqueline Novogratz, n.d. "CNN: Dambisa Moyo & Jacqueline Novogratz debate the efficacy of foreign aid." Online: http://www.youtube.com/watch?v=iCCWoJX2LM.

Munene, Alice, 2000. "The Gospel and African Belief in Spirits: A Correlative Study Based on African Instituted Churches and African Beliefs in Spirits." *Journal of African Cultures and Religion* 2 (2000) 69–78.

Musau, Paul M. "Polemics Versus Reality: Bridging the gap in Kiswahili research." In *Utafiti wa Kiswahili*, edited by Inyani K. Simala, 1–10. Eldoret: Moi University Press, 2002.

Mwinsheikhe, Halima Muhammed. "Using Kiswahili as a Medium of Instruction in Science Teaching in Tanzanian Secondary Schools." In *Language of Instruction in Tanzania and South Africa (LOITASA)*, edited by Birgit Brock-Utne et al., 129–48. Dar-es-Salaam: E and D, 2003.

Ntloedibe-Kuswani, Gomang Seratwa. "Witchcraft as a Challenge to Batswana Ideas of Community and Relationships." In *Imagining Evil: Witchcraft beliefs and accusations in contemporary Africa*, edited by Gerrie Ter Haar, 205–28. Trenton, NJ: Africa World Press, 2007.

Nyaga, Stephen Nyoka. "The Impact of Witchcraft Beliefs and Practices on the Socio-economic Development of the Abakwaya in Musoma Rural District, Tanzania." In *Imagining Evil: Witchcraft beliefs and accusations in contemporary Africa*, edited by Gerrie Ter Haar, 247–68. Trenton, NJ: Africa World Press, 2007.

Ocholla-Ayayo, A. B. C. *Traditional Ideology and Ethics Among the Southern Luo.* Uppsala: Scandinavian Institute of African Studies, 1976.

Odaga, Asenath Bole. "Christianity and the African Customary Practices." Maarifa Lecture given at Kima International School of Theology, Kenya, June 23, 2004.

Ogechi, Nathan Oyori. "The Reality and Challenges of Publishing in Kiswahili in Kenya." In *Utafiti wa Kiswahili*, edited by Inyani K. Simala, 25–35. Eldoret: Moi University Press, 2002.

Ogot, Bethwell A., 1999a. "Africa: The agenda of historical research and writing." In *Building on the Indigenous: Selected Essays 1981–1998,* 205–21. Kisumu: Anyange Press.

———, 1999b. "The Construction of Luo Identity and History" In *Building on the Indigenous: Selected Essays 1981–1998,*179–204. Kisumu: Anyange Press.

———, 1999c. "Building on the Indigenous: Reflections on culture and development in Africa." In *Building on the Indigenou: Selected Essays 1981–1998,* 137–45. Kisumu: Anyange Press.

Padilla, C.René. "Holistic Mission." In Lausanne Occasional Paper. (LOP). No. 33. *Holistic Mission,* edited by David Claydon (2005), 11–23. Lausanne Committee for World Evangelization, Pattaya, Thailand, September 29 to October 5, 2004. Online: http //lausanne.org/documents/2004forum/LOP33_IG4.pdf.

P'bitek, Okot. *African Religions in Western Scholarship.* Nairobi: East African Literature Bureau, 1970.

———. *Religion of the Central Luo.* Nairobi: East African Literature Bureau, 1971.

Pennycock, Alastair. *The Cultural Politics of English as an International Language.* London: Longman, 1994.

———. *English and the Discourses of Colonialism.* London: Routledge, 1998.

Prah, Kwesi Kwaa. "Going Native: Language of instruction for education development and African emancipation." In *Language of Instruction in Tanzania and South Africa (LOITASA),* edited by Birgit Brock-Utne et al., 14–34. Dar-es-Salaam: E and D, 2003.

Puja, Grace Khwaya. "Kiswahili and Higher Education in Tanzania: Reflections based on a sociological study from three Tanzanian university campuses." In *Language of Instruction in Tanzania and South Africa (LOITASA),* edited by Birgit Brock-Utne et al. Dar-es-Salaam: E and D, 2003.

Qorro, Martha A. S. "Unlocking Language Forts: Language of instruction in post-primary education in Africa—with special reference to Tanzania." In *Language of Instruction in Tanzania and South Africa (LOITASA)*, edited by Birgit Brock-Utne et al., 187–96. Dar-es-Salaam: E and D, 2003.

Rassool, Naz. *Global Issues in Language, Education and Development: Perspectives from postcolonial countries.* Clevedon: Multilingual Matters, 2007.

Reed, Lawrence W., n.d. "Liberty Blossoms in East Africa." Online: http://www.isil.org/resources/fnn/2002mar/liberty-in-kenya .html.

Rowell, John. *To Give or Not to Give?: Rethinking dependency, restoring generosity and redefining sustainability.* London: Authentic, 2006.

Rubagumya, Casmir, M. "English Medium Primary Schools in Tanzania: A new linguistic market in education?" In *Language of Instruction in Tanzania and South Africa (LOITASA)*, edited by Birgit Brock-Utne et al., 149–69. Dar-es-Salaam: E and D, 2003.

Russo, John Paul. "Review of: After Babel: Aspects of Language and Translation by George Steiner." *Modern Philology* 76 (1979) 444–48.

Sachs, Jeffrey. "The End of the World As We Know It: The fight against extreme poverty can be won, but only if Bush recognises that military might alone won't secure the world." *Guardian,* April 5, 2005. Online: http://www.commondreams.org/views05/0405-26 .htm.

Singleton, Harry. "Between Racism and Obscurity: The black theologian in the twenty-first century." *Black Theology: An International Journal* 6 (2008) 12–31.

Seidlhofer, Barbara, ed. *Controversies in Applied Linguistics.* Oxford: Oxford University Press, 2003.

Simiyu, Oliver Kisaka. "Raising Leaders of Integrity." *AICMAR Bulletin* 8 (2009) 29–44.

Southall, Aidan W. "Social Anthropology and East African Development." *Mawazo* 1 (1968) 52–56.

———. *Alur Society: A Study in Processes and Types of Domination.* London: Oxford University Press, 1970.

Sperber, Dan, and Deirdre Wilson. *Relevance: Communication and Cognition.* 2nd ed. Oxford: Blackwell, 1995.

Steiner, George. *After Babel. Aspects of Language and Translation.* 3rd ed. Oxford: Oxford University Press, 1998.

Stinton, Diane B. *Jesus of Africa: Voices of Contemporary African Christology.* New York: Orbis Books, 2004.

Tempels, Placide. *Bantu Philosophy.* Paris: Presence Africaine, 1959.

Thiong'o, Ngugi wa. *Decolonising the Mind: The politics of language in African literature.* Nairobi: East African Educational Publishers, 1981.

Tshehla, Samuel M. "Can Anything Good come out of Africa? Reflections of a South African Mosotho Reader of the Bible." *Journal of African Christian Thought* 5 (2002) 15–24.

Van Beek, Walter E. A. "The Escalation of Witchcraft Accusations." In *Imagining Evil: Witchcraft beliefs and accusations in contemporary Africa,* edited by Gerrie Ter Haar, 293–315. Trenton, NJ: Africa World Press, 2007.

Venuti, Lawrence. *The Scandals of Translation: Towards an ethics of difference.* London: Routledge, 1998.

Weber, Max. *The Protestant Ethic and the Spirit of Capitalism.* London: George Allen and Unwin, 1930.

Whitelam, Keith W. *The Invention of Ancient Israel: The silencing of Palestinian history.* Abingdon: Routledge, 1996.